SOLUTION
to
NAXALISM

SOLUTION
to
NAXALISM

Dr PK Agrawal, IAS (Retd)

Manas Publications
(We Convert Fighters into Writers)
New Delhi - 110 002 (INDIA)

MANAS PUBLICATIONS
(We Convert Fighters into Writers)
(Publishers, Library Suppliers, Importers & Exporters)
4402/5-A, Ansari Road (Opp. HDFC Bank)
Darya Ganj, New Delhi - 110 002 (India)
Phones: Off.: 011-23260783, 23265523, Res.: 011-23842660
E-mail: manaspublications@gmail.com
manaspublications@yahoo.com
Website: www.manaspublications.in

ISBN 978-81-7049-521-5
₹ 595.00

Designed at
Manas Publications

Printed in India at
R.K. Printers, Delhi
and published by Mrs Suman Lata for
Manas Publications, 4402/5-A,
Ansari Road (Opp HDFC Bank),
Darya Ganj, New Delhi - 110002 (INDIA)

To

Mahasweta Devi

the Doyenne of Land Reforms

in India

Preface

Naxalism is the biggest challenge to the internal security of India. A day doesn't pass when an incident of violence by Naxalites is not reported or viewed on television. Naxalism is causing more casualties yearly than the terrorist violence in Jammu and Kashmir and militancy in North-Eastern States.

The government had been fighting a pitched battle with various groups of Naxalites for more than four decades but the problem has not yet been solved. In fact, total number of incidents and number of casualties had been continuously on increase except recently when the number of casualties in Naxalite violence has come down inspite of increase in number of total incidents. Therefore, people in general have a genuine cause of concern how the Naxalite violence can be reduced if it cannot be eliminated permanently.

Due to widening net of Naxalite violence to railway trains or tracks, common man in India feels threatened in respect of his security. Where there is injustice, violence will be its natural fallout, sooner or later. If an equitable or egalitarian society is established in true sense, there will be peace. The equity can be achieved either by liberal release of funds, goods and services by the State or by equitable redistribution of properties in the society. In rural India, most of the properties are locked in landed properties. Therefore, land reform for equitable redistribution of land is required. No government can afford to make largesse of state available to about 40 crore i.e 400 million rural poor below poverty line (BPL).

Land reform is the plank to take the country in the comity of developed countries. China has distributed its 90 per cent arable land among about 90 per cent landless families or households. So, also in Japan, 41 per cent available arable land has been distributed among 81 per cent landless families. In India, as per an estimate by Roy Prosterman of Rural Development Institute and University of Washington, USA, only about 5 per cent land has been distributed among less than 28 per cent of the landless persons. Thus, there is a wide gap of inequality existing in India and lot of work is still required to be done.

When the need for land reform is projected before the bureaucrats or politicians concerned, there is lukewarm response. The new crop of bureaucrats incharge of implementation of land reforms either doesn't understand the land reforms or they don't have any willingness to understand under the influence of globalization which will collapse after sometime. Over and above, the police personnel as usual, assure to the bureaucrats and political bosses, that they will soon overpower Naxalites and restore peace and order in the society which never happen. The political executives don't want to venture to implement land reforms, because firstly, their field level cadres or supporters either don't appreciate the benefits of land reforms in long run or they don't want to disturb the *status quo* in rural India though rural society is sitting on a volcano of unrest. The Naxalites while spreading their cult of violence, project such cases of palpable injustice and discrimination before the downtrodden people and assure them to undo long injustice caused to them with their armed might. The simple and innocent poor villagers are easily carried away by their propaganda. A section of villagers, who do not toe their line, are either threatened or victimized. They do not find any protection from the local police in the face of threat of Naxalites in villages. Accordingly, they also succumb to their influence.

The rural poor know only technology of cultivation. If they are put back into cultivation, they will not starve. If they are evicted from cultivation due to land acquisition, they will be jobless and will swell the ranks of the poor after the hefty compensation received by them for their dear land is exhausted. Therefore, there is so much agitation by the land evictees against tinkering of their new favourable Land Acquisition Act.

It is a fact that the police in various States, is trying their best to tackle Naxalite violence. Para-military forces have been deputed in large numbers by the Central Government in the affected States to prevent violence by the Naxalites. There is some success here and there. At present, the Naxal violence has come down. Many Naxalites have surrendered yet problem re-appears in some other States in aggravated form. Andhra Pradesh has controlled the Naxal violence by creating new specialized commando force specialized in jungle warfare named Greyhounds, yet the problem is not over.

But in Andhra Pradesh also, the counter violence by police and Greyhounds was accompanied with extensive land reform measures undertaken by popular late Chief Minister YSR Reddy. In West Bengal, there was no Naxal violence during long 31 years regime of Left Front government from 1977 to 2008 because the main agenda of the Left Front government was implementation of land reforms. It was only in the year 2008, when the Left Front government gave priority to land acquisition for industrialization over land reforms specially in Singur and Nandigram areas. The flare-up thereby caused could not be controlled by the powerful Left Front government in West Bengal and it was dethroned from power in the year 2012. Various State Governments are trying in their own ways to wean away the rural poor from the Naxal fold like the Chhattisgarh Government has been providing rice in tribal areas on a very concessional rates and sustained brainwashing campaign.

Similarly, implementation of STORFA, 2006 is a good step to ensure right to land in the vicinity of forests under occupation by tribals etc and to ensure right to collect minor forest produce like woodlots, fallen leaves and dry jungle seeds and flowers. However, concerted efforts have yet to be undertaken so that there may be direct impact on the campaign of Naxalites who have also derailed from their main track of land reforms. Now-a-days, Naxalites are engaged only to counter the powerful State police force and they have been virtually left with no time or opportunity to pay to their main agenda to ensure land to the landless and the tiller, delivery of justice to the poor etc.

If government surplus land is not available for distribution, government should purchase land in the same village or neighbouring village where the landless poorest of the poor will go and cultivate the land and will save himself and his family from starvation. The government should distribute minimum 16 decimal land per family for three-tier cultivation starting from coarse grain cultivation and vegetable cash crops to fast growing trees as in Bangladesh.

In Jharkhand, government surplus ceiling land should be distributed among the landless persons specially the tribals on priority. In Chhattisgarh, all land including unsurveyed land of Abujmarh area in erstwhile Bastar district covering more than 5,000 ha should be surveyed and updated computerized land records should be made and distributed to all landowners and Pattadars. In the State of Odisha, Bataidars (sharecroppers) should be recorded on land which have been cultivated by them on the promise or by convention to share produce. In Madhya Pradesh, the tribals living on the fringe of forests should be recorded and given right to collect minor forest produce or dry leaves under the STORFA, 2006. Karnataka presents a scenario, where contract farming can be utilized for the advantage of the farmers whose lands have been given for contract farming. Uttar Pradesh highlights a scene where land acquired for large public sector enterprises is still lying vacant and is a source of problem for the units as well as for local people.

In Andhra Pradesh, land is required to be restored to the tribals which was illegally transferred to non-tribals. In Andhra Pradesh, Nyaya Panchayats at the block level or at Panchayat Samiti is an innovation worth emulation by other States. In Bihar, land records are almost non-existent, inspite of availability of requisite fund by the Central Government for the purpose. There is an urgent need for updation of land records and vesting of surplus land in government belonging to erstwhile Zamindars or Jotedars. In West Bengal, large quantum of land is locked in court cases specially in High Court and the Supreme Court which can be distributed, if released from Courts, among the landless poor persons. In Maharashtra, lack of bank finance for the crops is the main cause of suicides by the farmers specially in Vidarbha region of Maharashtra.

The police solution is underway in all affected States of India. There are some stories of success of the police operation like Greyhounds in Andhra Pradesh, Auxiliary Armed Police Force in Chhattisgarh, killing of top Naxalite leader in genuine police encounter in West Bengal, 40 per cent recruitment in Central Para-military forces from border areas and areas affected by militancy or Naxalism. However, due 'political will' to solve the Naxalite problem by the State Governments has not yet been demonstrated.

Due to traditional anti-people working of police, the police action could not make perceptible change in the situation. There is more of blame game between the local police and deployed para-military forces, posting of unwilling officers in those areas rather than the cream of officers from the State police force, incidents of connivance of local police with Naxalites and lack of actionable intelligence information by local police set-up and inadequate bank of knowledge about local inhospitable terrain with the local police. Even if all deficiencies are removed in the police set-up, it will not be able to solve the problem unless concerted efforts are made through implementation of land reform measures and development schemes in an impartial manner. Developmental schemes afflicted with corruption fuel the Naxalite agitation more than they solve. But development schemes cannot be stopped for that reason. There should be many times more vigilance on execution of developmental schemes in Naxal-affected areas than elsewhere in the country.

I am sure that the Indian administration led by the political executives will awake and undertake implementation of land reform measures in the Naxal-affected States on top priority basis. This book will be helpful to the policy-makers, ministers, administrators, Panchayat representatives, academicians and others to solve the problem of Naxalism in India on permanent basis.

I am thankful to the publisher of this book ie Manas Publications who have undertaken a mission to publish such books in the interest of our nation.

Dr PK Agrawal

Contents

1

Policy of NDA Government to Tackle Naxalism

The NDA government came to power in 2014 under the Prime Ministership of Narendra Modi. This government has slightly different policy to tackle Naxalism from the earlier UPA government who had declared the policy through Status Paper on the Naxal Problem on 31st October 2006. The NDA government terms Naxalism as Left Wing Extremism (LWE) on the basis of their ideology.

The Central Government has adopted an integrated four-points approach to address the Naxal problem in the areas of security, development, enforcing rights and entitlements of local communities, public perception management and good governance.

Approach of the Government of India

The government's approach is to deal with Naxalism in a holistic manner, in the areas of security, development, ensuring rights and entitlements of local communities, improvement in governance and public perception management. In dealing with this decades-old problem, it has been felt appropriate, after various high-level deliberations and interactions with the State Governments concerned, that an integrated approach specially aimed at the relatively more affected areas would deliver results. With this in view, a detailed analysis of the spread and trends in respect of Naxal violence has been made and 106 districts in ten States have been taken up for special attention with regard to planning, implementation and monitoring various interventions. However, 'Police' and 'Public Order' being State subjects, action on maintenance of law and order lies primarily in the domain of the State Governments. The Central Government closely monitors the situation and supplements and coordinates their efforts in several ways. These include providing Central Armed Police Forces (CAPFs) and Commando Battalions for Resolute Action (CoBRA); sanction of India Reserve (IR) battalions, setting up of Counter Insurgency and Anti-Terrorism (CIAT) schools; modernization and upgradation of the State Police and their intelligence apparatus under the scheme for Modernization of State Police Forces (MPF) scheme; re-imbursement of security related expenditure under the Security Related Expenditure (SRE) scheme; filling up critical infrastructure gaps under the Scheme for Special Infrastructure in Left Wing Extremism-Affected States; providing helicopters for anti-Naxal operations, assistance in training of State Police through the Ministry of Defence, the Central Police Organisations and the Bureau of Police Research and Development; sharing of intelligence; facilitating inter-State coordination; assistance in community policing and civic action programmes etc. The underlying philosophy is to enhance the capacity of the State Governments to tackle the Maoist menace in a concerted manner. The Ministry also monitors the implementation of Integrated Action Plan for LWE-Affected Districts (now called Additional Central Assistance to Naxal-Affected Districts) and various other development and infrastructure initiatives of Government of India.

Review and Monitoring Mechanisms

A number of review and monitoring mechanisms have been established by the Government of India in this regard. They include:

- A Standing Committee of the Chief Ministers of the LWE-Affected States under the chairmanship of the Union Home Minister, to work out a coordinated policy and specific measures to deal with the Left Wing Extremism problem on the political, security and development fronts.
- Review Group (earlier called the Task Force) under the Cabinet Secretary to review coordinated efforts across a range of development and security measures.
- An Empowered Group of Officers, headed by the Member-Secretary Planning Commission, with officers from the development Ministries and the Planning Commission, to oversee effective implementation of development schemes in Left Wing Extremism-Affected States.
- An Empowered Committee under Additional Secretary (LWE) to review the progress of various developmental

schemes/projects, with the Joint Secretary (LWE) and the Joint Secretary of the concerned ministries.

Schemes for Naxal-Affected States

Security Related Expenditure (SRE) Scheme

Under the Security Related Expenditure (SRE) scheme, funds are provided for meeting the recurring expenditure relating to insurance, training and operational needs of the security forces, rehabilitation of Left Wing Extremist cadres who surrender in accordance with the surrender and rehabilitation policy of the State Government concerned, community policing, security-related infrastructure for village defence committees and publicity material.

Special Infrastructure Scheme (SIS)

The Scheme for Special Infrastructure in Left Wing Extremism-Affected States was approved in the Eleventh Plan, with an allocation of ₹500 crore, to cater to critical infrastructure gaps, which cannot be covered under the existing schemes. These relate to requirements of mobility for the police/security forces by upgrading existing roads/tracks in inaccessible areas, providing secure camping grounds and helipads at strategic locations in remote and interior areas, measures to enhance security in respect of police stations/outposts located in vulnerable areas etc. This scheme was expanded to provide funds for upgradation of infrastructure, weaponry, equipment and training of Special Forces of LWE-Affected States. From financial year 2015-16, the Scheme has been transferred to States as per budget provisions of Ministry of Finance.

Additional Central Assistance to LWE-Affected Districts (Earlier Integrated Action Plan—IAP)

The Planning Commission has been implementing Integrated Action Plan (IAP) now Additional Central Assistance (ACA) for 82 selected tribal and backward districts for accelerated development. The aim of this initiative is to provide public infrastructure and services in 82 affected/contiguous districts. Originally, a sum of ₹25 crore and ₹30 crore was released to 60 districts during the financial years 2010-11 and 2011-12 respectively. This scheme has now been extended to 22 more LWE-affected districts, taking the total coverage to 82 districts. The nature of major works/projects taken up by the districts under the IAP include construction of school buildings/school furniture, Anganwadi centres, drinking water facilities, rural roads, Panchayat Bhawan/community hall, godowns/PDS shops, livelihood activities, skill development/training, minor irrigation works, electric lighting, health centres/facilities, Ashram Schools, construction of toilets, construction of multi-purpose Chabutara, construction of passenger waiting hall, special coaching classes for students, construction of ANM Centres, development of playgrounds, etc. The scheme is being continued as 'Additional Central Assistance to LWE-affected districts' with an increased coverage of 88 districts during the financial years 2013-14 and 2014-15. Under this scheme, a total number of 1,34,065 projects have been completed till 10th July 2015. The scheme has been transferred to States from financial year 2015-16.

Road Requirement Plan for Naxal Areas

The Road Requirement Plan (RRP) Phase-I was approved in February 2009 for improvement of road connectivity in 34

LWE-affected districts in 8 States viz Andhra Pradesh and Telangana, Bihar, Chhattisgarh, Jharkhand, Madhya Pradesh, Maharashtra, Odisha and Uttar Pradesh. The RRP-I envisages development of 1,126 kms of National Highways and 4,351 kms of State Roads (total 5,477 kms), at a cost of ₹7,300 crore. A length of 3,700 kms has been built at an expenditure of ₹4,946 crore till 1st June 2015.

Installation of Mobile Towers

The Cabinet, in its meeting held on 20th August 2014, has approved mobile towers at 2,199 locations, identified by the MHA in consultation with BSNL/State Governments in the 10 Naxal-affected States. Towers have started radiating at 363 locations as on April 1, 2015 with Andhra Pradesh (3), Chhattisgarh (351), Maharashtra (3) and Madhya Pradesh (6).

Scheme of Fortified Police Stations (PSs)

The Ministry has sanctioned 400 police stations in 10 Naxal-affected States at a unit cost ₹2 crore under this scheme. A total of 200 of PSs have been completed and work at 196 PSs is under progress up to 3rd July 2015.

Civic Action Programme

Under this scheme, financial grants are sanctioned to CAPFs to undertake civic action in the affected States. The idea is to win the hears and minds of local communities through small development schemes, which to some extent will mitigate the problems of people living in insurgency hit areas and also bring goodwill.

Ministry of Home Affairs

MHA is monitoring the situation on a regular basis at various levels. Home Minister reviews periodically convened meeting of the Chief Ministers of Chhattisgarh, Telangana, Odisha, Maharashtra and Jharkhand with specially 3 worst affected districts of Sukma, Bijapur and Dantewada of Chhattisgarh. Home Minister visited Chhattisgarh on May 30-31, 2015. Meetings are taken periodically by Home Secretary with State Chief Secretaries, DGPs and the Union Ministries/Departments, DIB, DGs of the CAPFs etc on critical and important issues in order to get better operational results and speeding up the development process.

- A Unified Command has been set-up in the States of Chhattisgarh, Jharkhand, Odisha and West Bengal. The Unified Command have officers from the security establishment, besides civilian officers representing the civil administration and it will carry out carefully planned counter Naxal measures.
- The Central Government approved a new scheme to assist the State Governments for construction/ strengthening of 400 fortified police stations at a cost of ₹2 crore each in Naxal-affected districts on 80 : 20 basis.
- An Empowered Group of Officers was set-up at the level of the Central Government to override or modify existing instructions on implementation of various development programmes and flagship schemes, having regard to the local needs and conditions in Naxal-affected areas for accelerated development.

- The Left Wing Extremism-affected States have been asked to effectively implement the provisions of the Panchayats Extension to the Scheduled Areas (PESA) Act, 1996 on priority, which categorically assigns rights over minor forest produce to the Gram Sabhas.

Conclusion

It is the belief of the Government of India that through a holistic approach focusing on development and security related interventions, the LWE problem can be successfully tackled. However, it is clear that the Maoists do not want root causes like underdevelopment to be addressed in a meaningful manner since they resort to targeting school buildings, roads, railways, bridges, health infrastructure, communication facilities etc in a major way. They wish to keep the population in their areas of influence marginalized to perpetuate their outdated ideology. Consequently, the process of development has been set back by decades in many parts of the country under LWE influence. This needs to be recognised by the civil society and the media to build pressure on the Maoists to eschew violence, join the mainstream and recognize the fact that the socio-economic and political dynamics and aspirations of 21st century India are far removed from the Maoist world-view. Further, an ideology based on violence and annihilation is doomed to fail in a democracy which offers legitimate forums of grievance redressal.

Reference

Source: www.mha.nic.in as on 19th August 2015.

2

Way Out to Tackle Naxalism

The status paper on Naxal problem issued by the Ministry of Home Affairs in the year 2006 by UPA government and four-points strategy adopted by NDA government are more or less similar. Both policies are brainchild of mandarins, located in old stony North Block, Ministry of Home Affairs, who are surrounded by Police Officers who have done only law and order work. As such both approaches have branded the problem as the 'internal security problem' and its solutions suggested are law and order centric. What else can they think of?

Common Strategy

The common strategy of both governments to deal with the problem of Naxalism has the following main features:

1. The Centre will fund the Naxal-affected States for modernization of the State police for sophisticated and latest telecommunication equipments and network by construction of more mobile towers and sophisticated

weaponry if not superior to the weaponry used by the Naxalites in the vulnerable police stations.

2. The Centre has undertaken to reimburse recurring security related expenditure (SRE) on rehabilitation and resettlement of Naxalite cadres, community policing, expenditure on village defence communities like Salwa Judum in Bastar, Chhattisgarh. Central Government also reimburses expenditure incurred on publicity to counter propaganda perpetuated by Naxalites and to seek cooperation from the civil society and the media.
3. **Additional Central Assistance (ACA)** has been earmarked to Naxal-affected districts to improve public infrastructure and services in Naxal-affected areas like construction of school buildings, school furniture, Anganwadi centres, drinking water facilities, rural roads, Panchayat Bhawans/community halls, godowns/ PDS shops, livelihood activities, skill development/ training, minor irrigation works, electric lighting, health centre facilities, Ashram Schools, construction of toilets, construction of multi-purpose Chaupals, construction of passenger waiting halls, special coaching classes for students, construction of ANM Centres, development of playgrounds etc. There is hardly any development issue which is left out. Only tardy implementation has to be made speedy and foolproof and which is the entire responsibility of the State Governments.
4. **Road Requirement Plan (RRP)** has been approved for improvement of road connectivity in 34 extremely Naxal-affected districts in States viz, Andhra Pradesh, Bihar, Chhattisgarh, Jharkhand, Madhya Pradesh,

Maharashtra, Odisha and Uttar Pradesh. This will meet the often repeated complaint by the security forces regarding problems faced by them in their mobility due to lack of roads in their campaign against Naxalites.

5. The Centre has sanctioned 400 new fortified police stations in Naxal-affected States at a cost of ₹2 crore each. Two hundred of them have already been constructed.
6. Distribution of title of the land to the tribals in the fringe areas of the forests where they have been residing for generations under the Scheduled Tribe and other Traditional Forest Dwellers (Recognition of Forest Rights) Act, 2006 in Naxal-affected areas on priority. Projects for development of social and physical infrastructure up to 1 ha has been approved for non-forest purposes. The progress is very slow in this regard. Upgradation of kutcha road constructed prior to 1 September 1980 has also been approved. Both governments also professed for speedy implementation of the Panchayats (Extension to Scheduled Areas) Act (PESA), 1986 to ensure *inter alia* that tribals can access to minor forest produce.
7. **Monitoring Mechanism:** The Indian administration has been leading in the world in regard to monitoring mechanism. In case of Naxal problem, the mechanism is perfect in three tiers:
   (i) There is a Standing Committee of the Chief Ministers of the Naxal-affected States under the Chairmanship of the Union Home Minister for

periodic review of policy and measures on the political, security and development fronts.

(ii) Review Group under the Cabinet Secretary to review quarterly developmental and security related works with the concerned Central Government Secretaries, Chief Secretaries and Director General of Police of affected States.

(iii) Monthly review by the concerned Chief Secretary of the concerned State with the DGP and Secretaries of development departments of the States. Joint Secretary from the Home Ministry may attend these reviews in the States.

Difference in Approach

(i) The Congress government led by Prime Minister Manmohan Singh had also taken into consideration that the Naxal groups had been raising mainly land and livelihood related issues. If the land reforms are taken up on priority and the landless and the poor in the Naxal areas are allotted surplus land, this would go a long way in tackling the developmental aspects of the Naxal problem. The States were accordingly requested to focus greater attention on this area as also to accelerate people centric developmental activities and create employment opportunities in the Naxal-affected areas. Thus implementation of land reforms was recognized as one of the strategies to fight against Naxalism whereas the present NDA government is silent about it.

(ii) There would be no peace dialogue by the affected States with the Naxal groups unless the latter agree to give up violence and arms as per earlier UPA-II government. The present government is silent about it.

(iii) The earlier UPA government was keen to promote voluntary local resistance group like Salwa Judum against Naxalites but the present government is only confining to creation of village defence parties.

(iv) The UPA government had asked the States to announce a suitable transfer policy for the Naxal-affected districts. Willing, committed and competent officers will need to be posted with a stable tenure in the Naxal-affected districts. These officers will also need to be given greater delegation and flexibility to deliver better and step up government presence and above all improve governance in these areas. Proper rewards for them were devised. The States generally pay no heed to such directives or advisories by the Central Government. The present NDA government is silent about it but has also not superseded the earlier order. Therefore, it can be presumed that this good practice will continue in the affected States.

(v) On the other hand as distinct from the erstwhile UPA government at the Centre, the present government is committed to win the hearts and minds of local communities through small development schemes which to some extent will mitigate the problems of people living in insurgency hit areas which will also earn goodwill to security forces. The present government recognizes the fact that the socio-economic and political dynamics and aspirations of 21st century India are far removed from the Maoist world-view. Further, an ideology based on violence and annihilation is doomed to fail in democracy which offers legitimate forums of grievance redressal. It is therefore, hoped that the present government will launch a concerted move to brainwash local people and Naxals to abjure violence at the national level and at the local level.

(vi) **Suggested Strategy:** Apart from foregoing strategy by two recent successive governments at the Centre, the additional solutions to tackle Naxalism can be divided in following two categories.

(a) Police Solution

The governments at the Centre and in States are well-equipped to tackle Naxalites through violence by the State. The State in this nuclear age is so powerful that there is hardly a possibility of revolution. Conditions like cultural revolution in China no longer exist in India. However the Indian army has rightly declined to participate in operations against Naxalites as these are all internal security operations except that they get some supplies of arms from foreign agents or terrorist groups who are interested to make India unstable. The Indian para-military forces like BSF and ITBP have been successfully guarding the international borders of the country. They can be any time called in when the situation goes out of control of the local police and local para-military forces like CRPF (Central Reserve Police Force). Even then the police response can be improved to tackle Naxalism in following ways:

(a) The local police and the deputed central para-military force should be trained in Guerilla Warfare though it is difficult because the security force can never match the local knowledge and expertise of terrain and also of local populace. This remains a gap and therefore, sometimes causalities on the side of security forces are unusually high because the Naxalites use hit and run tactics to inflict heavy causalities on the side of security forces and to run away with their sophisticated arms and ammunition left over. The security forces are given small funds to meet small development needs of local people like drinking water etc. It is not assessed how much success has been achieved by this step. But this is a good steps as the security forces are best suited to fulfil those needs which will have local support to the security forces.

(b) The government is not apt in the art of counter propaganda which is a must to counter anti-government or any propaganda by strongly doctrinated group like Naxalites. No propaganda can be effective unless it is highly exaggerated or partially false. A government officer doing that job can be subsequently held personally liable in departmental action against him for violating code of conduct of his service. Can a blast on railway track killing hundreds of people not make a catchy propaganda?

(c) The anti-Naxalite forces lack in perfect intelligence as the movement of Naxalite is very fast and local people are with them either internally or due to fear of reprisals by the Naxalites. The informers of police cannot move so fast due to inhospitable terrain or jungles. There is lack of co-ordination among intelligence network of various police agencies and its mutual exchange and mutual trust.

(d) The counter insurgent forces require familiarity with the local culture, local mores and language. The local police is sometimes not very cooperative. Few among them may be sympathizers of the local insurgent elements like Naxalites. That creates, a gap between the local population and security forces. Sometimes, a small action or inaction of conduct by them towards innocent local youths, girls or women can trigger violent demonstration by the local people.

(e) There is lack of co-ordination among States. The Naxalites use this to their advantage and cross over the borders after doing some big incident in one State through the inter-connected jungles known as Red Corridors which know no borders. It has been observed so far that after a major incident in one State, the Naxalites were not arrested by government in another State.

(f) Some States had innovative measure, like Andhra Pradesh which has founded the anti-Naxal police force known as Greyhounds team or squads. This team or force was adept in jungle warfare, though this force had an initial casualty of more than 37 of its men, yet it has proved very effective and "there has been a decline of 40 per cent in Maoist violence activities since its formation by the Andhra Pradesh Government."[1] Andhra Pradesh has been able to control the Naxal violence to a great extent. Other States don't follow these innovative tactics by their neighbouring States until the Central Government asks them to follow and provide them fund to equip them for the fight against Naxalism. Thus, the affected States have to manage their financial resources well so that they can find out their own resources to fight Naxalism locally through the use of their local tactics and strategy. It is becoming a bad fashion that State blames the Centre for all ills but begs the Centre for help in all matters from money to man.

(g) There is no definite policy to post police personnel in Naxal zones. The police officers are posted as a matter of punishment, though the best of the lot of police officers should be posted in these areas as this is the most critical problem of the present age. As a result, the local force is led by unwilling officers at the top. Secondly, the local police personnel in league with Naxalites are not transferred and punished. The police inspectors and constables should be screened for their performance. After an incident, there should not only be an enquiry, but the results or finding of enquiry should also be implemented and the guilty should be punished immediately. In absence of such actions, sometimes senior police officers and number of personnel of para-military force are killed by the Naxalites using the information of their movement which causes demoralization in Central Security Force and terror in public. Due to such incidents, local people don't come forward to help police because they will be persecuted by the Naxalites. Thus, local people are surrounded between the Naxalites and the police, ie devil and the deep sea.

(h) The police should see that the surrendered Naxalites are given due police protection so that they are not killed by their rivals for surrendering to the police. The police should also follow up with the administration for proper rehabilitation of the surrendered Naxalites so that they are paid government declared grants without delay. This will build up faith and more Naxalites will surrender before security forces.

(i) The police is unable to protect their informers firstly because the insiders in the police force disclose their names and secondly because the police fails to give them due protection. If such a situation continues, people will not come forward to provide intelligence information to police and local assistance also. This will cause more casualties among security organizations.

The statistics reveal that lot of police informers are included among the civilians killed. This speaks poorly of the police force.

(j) The experiment of posting of 'special police officers' (SPOs) in Jammu zone has been very successful. "They have been contributing to the collecting and developing local intelligence, providing contingency pause to meet unforeseen situations and assisting police and para-military force in undertaking independent and joint anti-terrorist operations. The performance of SPOs has all along been commendable on the anti-military front and has also proved to be the backup support base to the Village Defence Committees."[2]

Union Home Minister Rajnath Singh is committed to constitute village defence committees in Naxal areas. These committees will be able to work smoothly provided they have backup of SPOs otherwise Naxalites will blow them over.

(k) When the Naxalites fail to come in limelight only by resorting to local violence, they resort to violence on railway tracks, railway stations, post offices, telephone exchanges and other central and State Government installations, the school buildings, Panchayat Bhavans etc.

It is seen that in-house police team of railways is not well-equipped to face the challenge of violence on railway track or on running trains. The Railway Ministry, being an independent organization, should strengthen and modernize RPF (Railway Protection Force) and GRP (Government Railway Police) in terms of manpower, training and weapons. The Railways, being a competent and financially sound organization, should set-up a credible mechanism to enable effective co-ordination on ground between RPF, GRP, local police intelligence agencies and even use space technology, for protection and safety of Railway passengers, trains, tracks and other railway properties. Railways have done a commendable technical solution by running a dummy engine during night before the Rajdhani trains and taking other running safety measures which have proved foolproof so far. More technical solutions are required for updation and change. However, Railway cannot do anything if Naxalites blow off some remote railway stations. If crores of passengers travelling in trains feel insecure, it will be a great insult to the law and order agencies of the country.

(l) Whenever there is violent flare-ups by Naxalites, the media covers it very well as a story without going into the depth. After the incident, the victims are taken care of by announcing compensation to the next kith and kin of the deceased persons and the injured persons. After that, everybody forgets, whether the compensation has reached the affected families or victims. Much less is taken care of the court cases registered in regard to the incident. The Naxalites involved are neither arrested nor they are prosecuted. Some encounters are reported later on but one cannot correlate them with gruesome incident. The way the Naxalites are prosecuted, is not made public. It is understandable that it is very difficult to investigate the cases against Naxalites as local witnesses are not available. Secondly, the Naxalites committing crimes hide their identities during commission of crimes. Thus, police administration has to gear up itself through a special cell which can prepare foolproof cases against Naxalite, which can stand judicial scrutiny. The solution doesn't lie in staging fake encounters in cases of arrested Naxalites like many in the past which will create more ill-will against police among Naxalites and public and will delay the solution of the problem.

(b) Developmental Solutions

The Naxalism has survived in India for almost 50 years. It shows that the solution of the Naxalism lies elsewhere. It is not simply an internal security problem. Its root cause is to be dug out and solutions be arrived at accordingly as permanent solutions. Mahasweta Devi (Padma Vibhushan), famous writer and ex-cultural ambassador of India, who worked for decades among tribals of Purulia district of West Bengal, commented on Jahanabad Jail-break of 2005 in Bihar,

> "The Naxalites are fighting for Adivasis and weaker sections of people. This fight for the poor is called 'Uggravad' (extremism) by those who lost the support of these poor people, but I call it a movement. Whether these (Naxals) are CPI(ML) or Naxalites, I want to pay my 'Salam' (salute) at this (old) age to Naxals who are fighting for the poor people."[3]

However, CPI(M) Politburo Chief Prakash Karat doesn't agree with Naxalites. He calls them misguided persons. Let us now analyse the gaps where the government can fill in by developmental solutions adopted by it—

(a) The developmental schemes are not being implemented properly. The annual expenditure on each scheme including modernization of police force is much below the target. In cases of developmental scheme, implemented through Panchayats like MNREGA, Integrated Tribal Development Programme, Backward Districts Initiative (BDI), the tribal Panchayat members do not exert as they are very simple people. They are either not eloquent to put up the cause of tribals in Panchayat meetings or their voice is not given proper heed to. There is corruption in Panchayat bodies also which find readymade issues in the hands of Naxalites to aggravate already aggrieved public. The corruption among local level officials like Lekhpal, Patwari, Talati, Police, further fuel the Naxalite agitation. Thirdly, in the Naxal-affected areas, the contractors work in a very hostile environment. The Naxalites extract money from them. Sometimes, the Naxalite don't allow developmental activities sponsored by the government under the fear that they will lose grip on the poor people. In such areas, naturally contractors can work only on much higher rates than the normal tender rates like emergency railway works. But audit objections are raised. As a result, the officers avoid giving work orders to undertake works in Naxal-affected areas. Something should be done to relax norms to implement government schemes in Naxal-affected areas where police cannot give twenty-four hour police protection to the development works.

(b) The 16-member expert group headed by D Bandyopadhyay on 'Development Issues to Deal with Causes of Discontent, Unrest and Extremism' has held that, "on the whole the approach of treating it as a law and order or a development problem is flawed."[4] The issue as per him is of denial of basic rights. The estimate of displacement of tribals under the land acquisition is huge and rehabilitation is poor. Accordingly, only 18-20 per cent tribals have been rehabilitated. In fact, upsurge of Naxalism in the second phase in 2009-10 in West Bengal was caused due to faulty land acquisition at Singur and Nandigram areas of the State.

Land reform has ten constituents which we may analyse how separately each constituent can be implemented in Naxal-affected States—

(i) **Distribution of government-vested land and giving possession to the Pattadars or assignees of the vested land:** This is a major factor. Most of the State Governments have poor performance. Sometime government/Panchayat land is not available in the village or in the vicinity. The tribals will not go very far to own and cultivate such land leaving his homestead. Therefore, government should purchase land for him and distribute at least 16 decimal of land so that a landless tribal or poor person may not die due to starvation and can cultivate himself to save himself and his family at least some vegetables, seasonal grains etc.

(ii) The landless persons are the poorest among the poor in tribal areas whom the Naxalites keep in front to demonstrate the poor performance and discrimination perpetrated by government after independence. Such persons should be given land on top priority basis. This should be done specially in Chhattisgarh, Jharkhand, Madhya Pradesh and Odisha on priority basis.

(iii) The sharecroppers or Bataidars should be recorded in land records i e records-of-right at least in the last column of comment, so that they may not be evicted on whims and fancies of the landowners whose land they have been cultivating for long. This can be done in Uttar Pradesh by executive order by Board of Revenue of Uttar Pradesh.

(iv) There is a need for continuous updation of land records and computerization as well. Lack of proper land records, in Bihar is the main cause of land disputes projected by Naxalites for which police has no answer or solution. Surprisingly, Abujmarh area of Bastar, Chhattisgarh spread over in about 5,000 ha has not yet been surveyed and placed on government record.

(v) Implementation of rural development schemes like MNREGA, ITDP and Water Harvesting schemes along with financial credit from banks for cultivation can help the poor farmers to stand on their legs. Then they will slowly be cut off from the Naxalite fold. This can be implemented speedily in Maharashtra and Karnataka.

(vi) Delivery of instant justice through the Lok Adalat by Naxalite on the spot has been very popular in Naxal villages in view of long pendency of litigation in regular forums. This can be countered by strengthening one of the components of land reforms ie availability of legal aid to the landless agricultural labourers, Pattadars, sharecroppers or poor peasants by holding dispute settlement camps on the pattern of Lok Jan Adalat by the Naxalites. This constituent can be implemented in Chhattisgarh and Jharkhand with much vigour and sincerity. Secondly Nyaya Panchayats may be constituted at least at Panchayat Samiti, block or Mandal level so that instant justice can be delivered to the villagers.

(vii) Allotment of house-sites and restoration of alienated tribal land can be implemented in Telangana and Andhra Pradesh to counter the influence of Naxalism in those two States apart from other States.

(viii) Social and religious reforms are required in all States as the poor persons waste their precious earning or government grants or subsidies on drinking and religious superstition specially in Andhra Pradesh, Jharkhand and Chhattisgarh. The NGOs and religious and charitable organizations can play vital role to tackle this problem among the poor specially tribals. The initiative by Prime Minister Narendra Modi (2015) for opening of bank accounts by all, to some extent has helped to create saving habit among poor persons.

(ix) The poor and the tribals are joining the Naxal fold because due efforts have not been made to organize them at the local level. Still it is not too late to organize them. They can be organized by the Panchayats or self-help groups in rural areas. Their waste-land can be cultivated by way of collective farming keeping the individual ownership intact and by implementation of various water harvesting schemes and land development schemes under various rural development schemes. Then from no production level out of the waste-land, they can get some production and their land will be cultivable or arable in near future. This was well-demonstrated by the Left Front government lead by CPI(M) in West Bengal from 1977 to 2011. Its main agenda was implementation of land reforms. It started the Operation Barga and involved full government machinery. About 14 lakh Bargadars or sharecroppers were recorded. West Bengal used to be most afflicted State by Naxalism. But after the Left Front government came in power in the late seventies (1977), the government also ensured distribution of government surplus land to the landless tribals, Scheduled Castes and others by holding Patta distribution camps under its rule. It also arranged crop finance by banks for them at concessional rate of interest, under the able leadership and guidance of its Land and Land Reforms Minister Benoy Krishna Chaudhary, who employed cream of officers for this work. The Pattadars were given possession and thus about 14 lakh landless persons were given land. The government ensured full support to Bargadars and Pattadars. As a result, administration was also developed and in the second phase of Naxalism in 2009-11, it was tackled by distribution of government surplus land by spirited officers in Naxal areas. Thus land reform is the only panacea which can provide permanent solution to the complex problem of Naxalism in ten States of India. It is not difficult. Similarly, implementation of land reforms is feasible in the whole country and requires following strategy:

(a) Firstly the new generation of politicians are neither trained nor they understand the land reform as institutional changes. They confuse themselves as if land reform is land improvement or increase in production. Therefore it is difficult to generate political will for undertaking land reforms. The Chief Minister alone cannot pilot the same. Secondly, the most unwanted or less powerful politicians and bureaucrats are posted to this all important department of revenue which has direct access to the last man in the society. As such, they cannot push the agenda of implementation of land reforms. Thirdly, political support up to the grass root level is required so that the lowest level revenue machinery implementing land reforms cannot be weaned away from the influence of local lobby of landowners, ex-Zamindars or Jagirdars and land mafia. Strong political will is required to direct police to protect officials involved in implementation of land reforms and not to undo what has been done by the land reforms machinery at the grass root level. Fourthly, the subordinate judiciary or quasi-judicial revenue courts should be trained and briefed how to protect the land reform beneficiaries and not to be misled by the fear and eloquent pleadings, from or on behalf of the landowners. The civil courts and lawyers should not be allowed to impinge upon this field.

(b) Thus, a proper mix of political will and administrative will be required so that land reform may be treated as sacrosanct and none should fiddle with it without valid cogent reasons. It is better if the functions of land reform or revenue officers on this account like ceiling etc are kept beyond purview of regular judicial courts. Fifthly, there is no dearth of funds available from Union Government. Department of Land Resources, Ministry of Rural Development is providing funds for updation of land records, aerial survey, development of waste-land etc. Even the Government of India is relaxing norms to provide funds for upgrading staff and affairs of Revenue Departments of State Governments which are used by State Governments for many other purposes like VIP duties by the Collector of the district except for their main duty of implementation of land reforms.

(c) Government should set-up a special vigilance machinery to check corruption in Naxal-affected districts specially with respect to schemes catering to counter the Naxalism. The grass root offices specially Gram Panchayat, Block Development Office, Sub-Registry Office should be specially kept under watch which have direct access to the villagers and ignite protest by Naxalites.

(d) The most affected villages should be ensured that these have drinking water facility, a school, Anganwadi centre and health facilities. The government officials who are responsible for such facilities should be held duly accountable. 'Chalta Hai' attitude is no longer acceptable and is irrelevant.

(e) As far as ideological war against Naxalism is concerned, it has to be started from the highest level of Home Minister of India down to the lowest level of Gram Panchayat. The NGOs or harbourers or financiers of Naxalites who foment violence by Naxalites should be brought to the book under law. High-handedness by the police should be avoided which will be counterproductive.

Conclusion

The ex-Union Home Minister P Chidambaram while addressing the Chief Ministers' Conference on Internal Security at New Delhi on 17th August 2009 gave a clarion call to the Naxalites:

> "Let our message to the Naxalites be this: We will talk, we will act, we will restore order and we will undertake development activities."[5]

Naxalites are also gradually losing public support because except delivery of instant justice through Lok Adalats, the Naxalites are doing nothing fruitful like restoration excess surplus government land from the clutches of land-owners and its distribution among the poor landless persons and restoration of cultivation by the sharecroppers, Bataiders, Bhagdars or Bargadars being evicted by the landowners on some pretext or the other. The Naxalites are engaged in running their organizations, collecting arms and ammunition and are doing fire-fighting like the security forces in retaliation or well-planned attacks to establish their dominance in the so-called liberated areas. The security forces are trying to keep them constantly on their toes inspite traversing in inhospitable and inaccessible terrain. Lot of precious government revenue is being spent by government to engage in battle like situation with its own people.

The popular governments have to care for dumb majority of the poor people including the landless persons and sharecroppers or who have now picked up arms against their double standards and the rest are in the process of taking up arms against the democratic governments. Land is the dearest asset to the villages. This is the permanent asset with them unlike assets created from other developmental schemes, which temporarily give them relief. Even, in this era of economic liberalization, the land is the most important issue in India. Even the votaries of globalization couldn't get the amendments in the New Land Acquisition Act, 2013 passed through by the present powerful Modi government though land acquisition is a secondary issue in the field of land reform. But this has brought fortunately the land reforms issues at the centre stage of the Indian polity. If the persons at the helm of affairs take the required measures with all earnestness, the existing availability of land in government land bank including land locked in various court cases will suffice for next ten years. But this has to be done in the mission mode approach unlike the routine revenue administration which is busy only in mutations and conversions of land and making land titles available mainly for the needs of industries and commerce. The revenue or land reform machinery has to arise, recognize their age-old friends or clients or stakeholders in villages and care for them as they are at present on the worst cross road of history.

REFERENCES

1. Uday Kumar: *Defeating Naxalite*, Lucky International, New Delhi, 2012, p 49.

2. Khoda, Kuldeep: "Police and Naxalism Combating Terrorism" in *Police and Naxalism: Strategies for Solutions*, ML Kumawat and Dr Nazral Islam (eds), Manas Publications, New Delhi, 2011, p 25.
3. Ibid 2: *Jansatta* (Hindi daily), Kolkata, 20 November 2005, p 34.
4. Ibid 1, p 140.
5. Ibid 2, p 171.

3

Strategy to Tackle Naxalism in Jharkhand

If any State that can be said to be fully afflicted with Naxalism, it is Jharkhand—the newly formed State from the erstwhile united Bihar. The solution regarding Naxalites problem in Bihar, *mutatis mutandis*, will apply to Jharkhand State. In fact most of the problems of Bihar have been inherited by the nascent State of Jharkhand. Since its inception, Jharkhand has become laboratory for the Naxals—a place for experimenting with the idea of establishing a parallel system of governance. The Naxals have transformed 16 out of the 22 districts of the State into a 'guerilla zone'. They include Garhwa, Palamau, Chatra, Hazaribagh, Giridih, Bokaro, Ranchi, Latehar, Lohardaga, Gumla, Simdega, East Singhbhum, West Singhbhum, Dhanbad, Sarakela-Kharswan and Kodarma. Implementation of land reform in Jharkhand is the key instrument to tackle Naxalism in the following way.

Updating of Land Records

Correct up-to-date records-of-right are crucial for the implementation of land reform.

Therefore, wherever the records are incorrect and not up-to-date, necessary steps should be taken to rectify and update them. For hill areas which have not been cadastral surveyed so far, a special programme for a cadastral survey will have to be initiated also apart from the normal survey and settlement operations, which may continue where they are already underway. Alternatively it can be done by way of digitalization of village maps through computers and integrating the village map with the individual plot of record-of-plots of each raiyat and updating of land records by engaging private vendors on computers where latest changes by way of mutation and conversions of land are invariably incorporated

Implementation of Ceiling Laws

The existing ceiling laws should be translated into the vernacular using simple language so that all concerned have a clear understanding of the implication of laws. Awareness, particularly amongst the beneficiaries, should be created by disseminating correct information through the audiovisual mass media. Benami transfers must be declared illegal, and such made in the past should be annulled and the land is vested in the government.

There should be some specific provisions in tenancy laws to precisely define and describe Benami transactions. Ledger of landholdings district-wise and block-wise need to be prepared by the methods of card indexing for effective implementation of ceiling laws.

List of big rural families should be drawn-up at the sub-divisional level and vigorous application of the ceiling laws initiated.

Then ceiling surplus government land should be distributed among the landless persons immediately so that none is left landless. If government requires to purchase land in remote areas specially Naxal-affected areas where ceiling surplus land is not available, government should give priority and purchase and distribute land among the landless persons giving priority to the tribals.

Recording of Sharecroppers

A crash programme of recording tenants or Bataidars should be undertaken on the pattern of recording of Bargardas in West Bengal. The tenant who is not tilling the land himself should be given an option, within a specific time, whether he would continue to cultivate the land himself otherwise *bona fide* cultivator for more than three years on his land should be recorded as sharecropper or Bataidar. In this respect, the recommendations of D Bandyopadhyay Committee should be implemented in phases.

Restoration of Land to the Tribals

Land transfers from tribals to non-tribals is not permitted. Even the Chhotanagpur Tenancy Act can be used to restore such land transfers to the non-tribals due to distress by the tribals. To restore confidence among the tribals, the pending cases of all those who have been illegally dispossessed or evicted should be disposed of expeditiously by summary trials in the time-bound programme. If necessary, additional special officers may also be deputed for the purpose. Cases which have been suppressed due to collusion with the staff should be examined as laid down in the Act and followed up.

If necessary, additional staff may be given. The onus of providing any right over the land which a non-tribal claims must be that of claimant. The Tribal Welfare Department staff should be posted in each block or Panchayat Samiti and may be utilized to identify cases of alienation and indebtedness.

The welfare staff should also pursue the cases of restoration and collusive title suits and take the follow-up action to give effect to the court's decision in case of tribals as friends, philosopher and guide of the tribals.

Mining and Restoration of Land to the Tribals

In case of land involved in mining, tribals should be allowed to cultivate on the surface of land wherever it is possible. After mining, the land should be restored to conserve environment and should be re-allotted to the tribals for whatever use they can do with that land. The representatives of the tribals are not vocal in Panchayat bodies for the cause of tribals. These gaps should be filled in by NGOs and other conscious persons or organizations.

People's Participation in Development Work

People's participation in land reform measures can be ensured through a committee constituted by nominated/elected representatives from amongst the members of the Scheduled Tribes living in that area or through sub-committees of Panchayat Samitis. Such committees should be formed at the Halka/block level for the sole purpose of implementing the aforesaid measures and should be kept active. All party consensus should be arrived at for speeding up the implementation process of land reform at the village level before the situation goes out of control. Infrastructure should be strengthened even at the cost of higher rates of work in the Naxal-affected areas. Farmer's pass book should be issued to all cultivators and landholders.

There should be regular arrangement of training of administrative personnel, concurrent evaluation of the quality of implementation of land reforms and development works mainly in tribal areas.

Area specific schemes should be drawn up based on local demand, local consultation and research with a view to fulfil the aspiration of the poorest of the poor in Jharkhand. Loopholes in implementation should be curbed. Corrupt officials, Panchayat representatives and political executives should be given exemplary punishment. The schemes undertaken to tackle Naxalism should be widely publicized in local newspapers, TV and also in the locality.

Justice delivery system at the grass root level should be initiated by constituting Nyaya Panchayats at the Panchayat Samiti/Block level. Above steps will help to bring the disgruntled youths in Jharkhand to the mainstream of the society.

4

Impact of Land Reforms on Naxalism in Chhattisgarh

More than 80 per cent of Chhattisgarh's population live in villages and most of the regions are affected by Naxalism. Only 12 per cent of the region's agricultural land is irrigated. The little irrigation facility that exists is limited only to the plain region. Hardly any irrigation is there in extremists' affected districts of Bastar which make serious headlines in the leading newspapers and are topics of heated discussions and debates. Inspite of stable government being voted by public, Naxalism has not been impacted upon what to say of a solution. Only fire-fighting solutions are going on by the police and security forces under the aegis of popular governments in power at the Centre and in the State.

In Chhattisgarh, the serious allegation is made that a large area of Abujmarh in Bastar and Narainpur districts covering more than 5,000 ha of land has not yet been surveyed and there is no land record for the same. In Madhya Pradesh and Chhattisgarh, the ownership of about 30 lakh acres of land is not yet ascertained. No government can justify, after 68 years of independence, that they cannot deliver the records-of-right to their citizens.

Secondly, the developmental activities of the tribal land through various schemes including MNREGA or through crop loans by the Banks are not reaching the tribals and they are still subject to exploitation by moneylenders. Thirdly, speedy judicial reddressal through courts or settlement of disputes through Nyaya Panchayats should be made available to them.

The implementation of land reforms thus is the only long-term as well as short-term solution which will address the following components:

1. Distribution of land to the landless under Land Ceiling Acts and ensuring possession of land to the allottees of the government-vested land.
2. Land alienation.
3. Non-recording of sharecroppers or Bataidar.
4. Land buying/grabbing by new landlords and exploitation of underground water by them.

The tribals have faith in local moneylenders and not in banks and co-operative institutions. They are further vulnerable to exploitation because of their innate cultural ethics of honesty and morality and their concern for the present instead for the future. The alienation of land by the tribals to the non-tribals for various reasons added to their woes. The Collector permitted alienation of agricultural land under the sham classification of non-agricultural land. Secondly, Collector did not apply adequate force to restore their land. The quantum of illegal (Benami) land alienation from tribals to non-tribals is like that part of the iceberg that remains under the surface of water.

The fundamental cause of giving tribal land to protect the tribals can be fully successful only if it is supplemented by measures to meet their genuine credit needs for cultivation including those for consumption and to protect them from usury. Secondly, the tribals having non-tribal land are equally vulnerable to exploitation. The judicial redress is not available to them unless they seek joint redress or go through legal aid system.

After orders passed in favour of tribals, non-tribals should be forcibly evicted from the land and the administration should ensure peaceful and effective possession of land to the tribals. There should be irrefutable presumption that the land shall belong to the original tribals unless it is obtained as per the provisions of law with the permission of the Collector.

The present legal measures to protect tribals from exploitation by moneylenders should be made more stringent and pro-active. Co-operative societies or government body should come to the protection of the tribals to take the burden of loan and ensure him delivery of land free from all encumbrances.

As per 1992 rural census of NSS, the total area leased in came to only 7 per cent of the area owned by all households. Thus, like Madhya Pradesh, Chhattisgarh is now a low tenancy State. However, there is 25 per cent of the total area under lease. Moreover the village level study of Lal Bahadur Shastri National Academy of Administration reports that sharecropping accounts for over 75 per cent of tenants and 65 per cent of the area is leased in.

The stagnation in agricultural productivity is of concern in the extremists' affected area. It shows that the productivity per landowner in the agricultural sector has not increased. There is need for more investment in the agricultural sector though the reduced size of farm has increased the number of marginal and small farmers. This is possible only through institutional financing of Pattadars and sharecroppers even though not recorded. Out of all divisions, Bilaspur division having Bastar district (undivided) has 75 per cent poverty as compared to 60 per cent in the State. The district is now divided into three districts namely Narainpur, Dantewla and Kanker. The rainfall is also inadequate. It is in few strong spells and, therefore, run off and evaporation are more. As a result in the absence of protective irrigation, the rice crop is highly prone to agricultural drought. A location specific strategy for extremists' affected areas has to be developed in Chhattisgarh. Total Watershed Planning (TWP) is one of the solutions. It will stabilize the natural resource house so as to facilitate its equitable and long-term use. Preservation of the natural base and ecology of these areas is the priority area for action.

Land Records Not Updated

The land records regarding the fact of cultivation are not updated for years. As a result, the farmers are denied access to credit, electricity or agricultural inputs and deprived of benefits of various anti-poverty programmes. The Panchayati Raj Institutions (PRIs) have to be more effective and assertive in collaboration with the local non-governmental or governmental bodies. If the vested interests in bureaucracy or elsewhere threaten them, they should face them with perseverance and sustainability. PRIs should ensure that they control Common Property Resources (CPR) like Naalas (drains), ponds, common grazing areas, outskirts if reserved for forests, barren and degraded forests and even forest produce which cannot be used otherwise by the forest officials of the government. The tribals living in forest areas will be given titles and they will be entitled to use forest produce without any fear or discrimination.

However, the State must not abandon its crucial role in protecting the cause of land reforms in these backward regions simply by handing over its pious responsibilities to PRIs and NGOs.

Salwa Judum[1]

Official version of the Salwa Judum portrays it as a people's struggle against the excesses of Naxalism. Villagers go to other villages and convince them to join. Many are attracted to join by the promise of payment of ₹1,500 per month, the weapon and the hope of getting permanent employment in the police force. But due to retaliatory action by the Maoists and mismanagement on the part of police administration, nearly 46,000 people were living in camps and abysmal conditions which the villagers do not like. They were to be settled in 581 new villages near roadside but the scheme could not get off the ground. Both sides claim civilian deaths. The government officers list 268 civilians killed (including some 50 SPOs) and 706 injured by the Maoists since June 2005. The Maoists have released a partial list of 116 civilians killed by the Salwa Judum till March 2006. In addition 72 police personnel and 30 Naxalites have died.

Leader of Salwa Judum Mahendra Karma told that it was the 'citizens' initiative' on the pattern of 'Bhumkal', the rebellion against the British, because the Maoist had singularly opposed modern development.

However, in its drive to establish their own 'Janta Sarkar', the Maoists have resisted even genuine government initiatives. The Maoists are dependent on contractors for funds and the contractors are dependent on Maoists to work in their areas.

Whatever may be the reality, the Salwa Judum campaigning brings out the fact that the Maoists' movement is not beyond public scrutiny. If they fail or go astray, another countervailing movement will arise and resist in their own courtyard. Thus, the Maoists have to be very cautious. Had they attended only to implementation of land reforms, their movement could have gone unchallenged. The government machinery is better equipped in doing developmental works and have unlimited resources.

This is high time that the government implements land reform measures without further delay in Chhattisgarh where the Maoists have lost focus of their main aim. However, in the democratic system like ours, violence neither by the Maoists nor by the Salwa Judum can be justified. A third path has to be carved out, sooner or later. After killing of Mahendra Karma by Naxalites, the Salwa Judum movement is on sharp decline.

Not only theoretically, the writer also met the persons in authority who mattered to implement the land reforms in Chhattisgarh to tackle Naxalism in the State. It was noticed that except the Director of Land Records in the State of Chhattisgarh, nobody could appreciate the problem in true perspective. This is the real problem. Whatever development works are undertaken, they cannot solve the problem in long term. Therefore, the persons in power ie political executives and administrative executives have to realize that they have to begin to tackle Naxalism in Chhattisgarh in true perspective by taking steps to implement the land reforms. I am sure it is not too late to implement this golden solution.

REFERENCE

1. Sundar, Nandi: "Bastar, Maoism and Salwa Judum", *EPW*, C Ram Manohar Reddy (ed), July 2006, pp 3187-3192, No 29, Mumbai.

5

Problems in Tackling Naxalism in Odisha

There were serious incidents of Naxal violence in Odisha. Malkangiri Collector R Vineel Krishna was abducted in February 2011 by the Maoists and was released by acceding to their terms and conditions. They also sunk a boat carrying 61 anti-Maoist Greyhound policemen of Andhra Pradesh. Thirty-eight of them were drowned.

Odisha has 19 Naxal-affected districts. Such is the seriousness of the problem. The solution lies in land reform measures to be undertaken in Odisha. Another problem in Odisha is the large-scale displacement of people due to mining projects, plantations, proposed setting up of large industries and rich farmers occupying land of large number of poor people. As per estimate by the Ekta Parishad[1] (an NGO), about 1.5 lakh people have been driven away from their land and forests.

Odisha has one of the poorest areas in the country where there have been maximum deaths due to hunger in districts like Kashipur, Lanjigarh and Kalahandi.

It is a commonly acknowledged fact that the Scheduled Castes now termed as Dalits and tribals are the most disadvantaged sections of the Odisha society. The increasing presence of Naxalites in areas dominated by Adivasis has geographical reason viz that the hills and forests of Central India earlier known as Dandkaranya are well-suited for roaming guerilla warfare. The present development process is demand-based. Unless the baby cries, none cares for it. None goes to the doorstep of a person who is in need of help. The needy has to go for help. As a result, the tribals and Scheduled Castes are left behind in the race of development though lot of funds flow for them.

Status of Implementation of Land Reforms in Odisha

Implementation of land reforms up to December 2007 (GoI Report).[2]

Area in acres

Returns			Area declared surplus	Area taken possession	Area distributed to individual beneficiaries
Filed	Disposed	Pending			
(1)	(2)	(3)	(4)	(5)	(6)
60335	60076	259	189979	171463	159546

Total number of beneficiaries	SC beneficiaries		ST beneficiaries	
	No	Area	No	Area
(7)	(8)	(9)	(10)	(11)
142959	48866	51136	53060	66303

(*Contd.*)

Other beneficiaries		Area declared surplus but not distributed	Total number of cases and area involved in litigation	
Number	Area		Area involved	Number of cases
(12)	(13)	(14)	(15)	(16)
41033	42094	29784	15051	288

Revenue courts		High Courts		Supreme Court	
Area	Number	Area	Number	Area	Number
(17)	(18)	(19)	(20)	(21)	(22)
7137	169	7014	116	123	3

Bhoodan Land

(Area in Acres)

Area not available for distribution			Total	Net area
Reserved/transferred for public purpose	Unfit for cultivation	Misc. reasons		
(23)	(24)	(25)	(26)	(27)
5025	2539	10061	27524	1889

(Area in lakh acres)

Area		
Donated	Distributed	Balance
6.39	5.80	0.59

Government Waste-Land

Area distributed in lakh acres	Number of beneficiaries
7.34	NR

Alienation and Restoration of Tribal Lands

(1)	(2)	(3)	(4)	(5)	(6)
Cases filed in the courts	Area	Cases disposed of by the courts	Area	Cases rejected	Area
1,05,491	1,04,742	1,04,644	1,03,556	43,213	46,677

(7)	(8)	(9)	(10)	(11)	(12)
Cases decided in favour of Tribals	Area	Cases in which land was restored to Tribals	Area	Cases pending in courts	Area
61,431	56,879	61,364	56,854	847	1,186

The track record of distribution of ceiling surplus land by Odisha government seems to be satisfactory. However, one fails to understand why 5,025 acres of land has been reserved for public purpose which is not in any other State. Secondly, 10,061 acres of land has not been distributed due to miscellaneous reasons or due to undisclosed reasons. Even land unfit for distribution viz 2,539 acres can be put for distribution. If the beneficiaries return or reject the land, then only it should be treated as unfit. This apart from 15,051 acres of land locked in litigation, about 17,500 acres can be additionally put to distribution in addition to other huge areas of land available for distribution under Bhoodan Land and government waste-land.

It is learnt that thousands of acres of land is with Shri Jagannathji Religious and Charitable Trust spread over in all districts. As this is a government managed trust, the cultivators of the land may be recorded as sharecroppers and they may be asked to give at least 25 per cent share to the Trust if the Trust provides no input for cultivation. But this land cannot be left uncared for. This should not in any case go into the hands of big landowners. The poor people are closer to God. Let them honestly cultivate the land and offer due share to Lord Jagannath. The Trust will have to undertake extensive land reform measures.

The worrisome point is that the land of tribal landowners is not vested to government. This cannot be the approach except in the North-Eastern States where community ownership is recognized as far as land of the tribal raiyats is concerned. The Government of Odisha is in the mainstream of the national life. They may make an amendment that the surplus land of the tribal landowners can only be distributed among the tribal beneficiaries. It will serve both ways and will balance the traditional and modern outlook towards landlessness among the tribals. Mostly the cultivable land of the Scheduled Castes and Scheduled Tribes are unrecorded. In many cases, land owned by the tribals is physically occupied and cultivated by non-tribals. Due to ignorance and lack of awareness of land laws, the tribals accept the claim over their land by the local dominant non-tribals.

Ambiguities

The next plank of land reform is conferment of right of cultivation or ownership on tenants.

In Odisha, 2.97 lakh tenants have been conferred ownership on 1.15 lakh acres of land, as in September 2006.[3]

This figure can also go up to a large extent as informal tenancy is in vogue in Odisha.

The Orissa Estate Abolition Act, 1951, aimed at abolition of all intermediary interests including mortgagees and lessees of such land. The Estate Abolition (Amendment) Act, 1972 was further enacted to extinguish outstanding estates.

But the implementation of land reform laws could not be successful due to sway of landowner class in the politics and in bureaucracy. As a result, the toiling masses in Odisha still migrate to many States in India as they do not have requisite quantum of land to hold on in their villages.

After observing the success of land reforms in the neighbouring State of West Bengal, efforts were made by the government from time to time to record sharecroppers or to distribute land among the landless persons, but in the final analysis proper impact could not be seen. Former Chief Minister of Odisha Biju Patnaik followed West Bengal model of land reforms and his son Naveen Patnaik, the present Chief Minister, is enjoying the rich legacy of his father for about last fifteen years.

Thus, the State of Odisha requires thorough review of land reform laws so that they can be implemented by the enlightened bureaucracy. The Panchayat institutions are also weak in Odisha. Unless the rural landless persons or sharecroppers are organized, no fruitful results can come out. The Panchayat bodies are also to be made truly representative and should be protected from the onslaught of the rural landowners.

It is of interest to note that in the districts of Koraput, Kalahandi, Balangir and Sambhalpur, more quantum of land has been distributed than in coastal districts. The tribals or the rural poor could not take full advantage of the same because it was not followed by financial assistance for their cultivation and government support to improve upon their dear land which is a must at the initial stage of allotment otherwise the beneficiaries will be tempted to lease out their land again, due to distress or inability to tide over the transitional vacuum of credit to cultivate them.

Informal Tenancy

In Odisha, raiyat rights have been conferred on more that 1.6 lakh temporary lessees. However, 'Sharecroppers' should be recognized as 'tenants' in the State tenancy legislation. A special drive should be undertaken to unearth informal tenancy and implementation of Fair Rent.

The village record is the most crucial tool for ensuring efficient implementation of either ceiling or tenancy laws. Hence, its proper maintenance is essential. As per a study in Kalahandi district,

> "The land in some of the cases was not in the physical possession of the allottees and was under forcible occupation by farmers of the higher castes. In certain cases after the physical possession was given, the area of land recorded was less than initially allotted."[4]

Some tribals are doing Podu cultivation on Patta land which cannot sustain their livelihood.

However, there was no perceptible change in social and economic status of the allottees of land because of their poverty and extremely bad quality of the land distributed to them.

The land records in Odisha require thorough updation through computerisation for which Central Government has placed lot of funds with the Revenue Department, Government of Odisha. Most of the funds are unutilized. This is the high time that land records are updated. As a result lot of concealed land will surface and will be available for distribution to a large number of Dalits and Adivasis in Odisha.

The opposition to land acquisition in Odisha also requires a thorough insight. If it is motivated by some vested interests led by a few NGOs, it should be overlooked by the government.

The Chasi Mulia Adivasi Sangh (CMAS) is the front Maoist organization in Odisha which indulges in killing and throat cutting of police informers and the local opponents. However, the people of Odisha have always reposed faith in Lord Jagannath, bureaucrats and political leaders who have contributed towards implementation of land reforms and have done developmental works. However, on interviewing the Principal Secretary of the Revenue Department in-charge of land reform, I found that the bureaucracy is not adequately equipped, trained or motivated to undertake land reforms except District Collector in Odisha here and there. Therefore, the onerous responsibility will have to be discharged by the present Chief Minister Naveen Patnaik who is forward looking and people-oriented leader and has clear mandate to protect people from Naxalite menace implementing land reforms in Odisha.

REFERENCES

1. Ekta Parishad: Internet
2. Government of India, Department of Land Resource: Quarterly Progress Report (Cumulative) on implementation of Land Ceiling Laws for the Quarter ending December 2007.
3. Government of India, Ministry of Rural Development: Annual Report, 2006-07, Annexure XLIX, p 258.
4. Lal Bahadur Shastri National Academy of Administration, Mussoorie: *Land Reforms in India: An Empirical Study*, 1989-90, Volume I, p 128.

6

Attaining Way Outs in Madhya Pradesh

Madhya Pradesh had about 6 crore population as per 2001 census. The Scheduled Tribe population is 1.22 crore which is 20.3 per cent of the State's population and Scheduled Caste population is 15.17 per cent. Madhya Pradesh is rich in forests. Tribals and forests are inseparable. Most of the tribals inhabit forest areas or the fringes of the forests. There are 14 forest-rich districts which are inhabited by almost 80 per cent of the tribal population. Madhya Pradesh has 20 per cent of the total forest cover in the country.

The districts which are mostly affected by the Naxalite activities are forest-rich districts like Balaghat, Mandla and Dindori. Mandla district has the famous Kanha National Park. Similarly, some portion of Jabalpur district covering forest-rich areas is also affected by the Naxal activities. The Government of Madhya Pradesh is requesting the Central Government to include five more districts in the list ie Sidhi, Singrauli, Shahdol, Umaria and Anuppur. It shows increasing concern of the Government of Madhya Pradesh to the Naxalite menace.

The villages covered by Naxalites are located in dense forest areas where the communication and transportation facilities are very poor. The Gond and Baiga people of these villages used to go for bamboo cutting and other work to Chandrapur district of Maharashtra and Bastar district (now Chhattisgarh) where they came in touch with the Naxalites who were active there. Secondly, the economy of the tribal areas cannot be imagined without forests. Therefore, in Madhya Pradesh we shall examine the Naxalism vis-a-vis forest management and how can forest management be made supportive to the tribal economy which will also be consistent with the preservation and maintenance of forests.

Forest Management

The social forestry failed in Madhya Pradesh so also farm forestry. However, Joint Forest Management (JFM) was to some extent successful with its 'care and share philosophy'. Fulfilment of livelihood needs of the poor and the tribals are the preconditions for the sustainability of natural resources. Therefore, the tribals will like and encourage 'trees of poor' which are essentially employment-generating trees, as they require labour for gathering and collection, as opposed to trees which are cleared-felled either to fill up government coffers or the bellies of the rich or forest mafia. The tribals worship such trees which help to sustain their livelihood needs. Therefore, in Madhya Pradesh land reforms will have another component of forest. This will also be applicable in other Naxalite areas which are forest- and tribal-dominated. This is borne by the fact that over 60 per cent of the country's forest cover is found in 187 tribal districts of India where about 8 per cent of national population lives."[1]

Let us examine how 'the Scheduled Tribes and other Traditional Forest Dwellers (Recognition of Forest Rights) Act, 2006 has been implemented.

The following problems are coming in the way of implementation of the provisions of the Act before the tribals can be handed over records-of-right for land in forests or fringes of the forests:

1. The tribals do not have proper caste certificates. Issuance of caste or tribe certificate is a Herculean job which is not possible for the simple and illiterate tribal to get from the respective sub-divisional officer and at present even from the common service centre.
2. The revenue machinery is not prepared to take up the responsibility of such a stupendous job of survey of all tribal areas near forests, the demarcation of land of each tribal or dweller and to prepare records-of-right for each individual raiyat or owner.
3. The forest officials without whose co-operation the Act cannot take off, are not mentally prepared to accept the primary position accorded to the tribals whom they used to treat like thieves or trespassers in the forests.
4. In some of the areas, Gram Sabhas are not convened. Then, how can the cases be cleared, remains to be answered. Without concurrence of Gram Sabha, Pattas in forest land cannot be given.
5. The Act is silent against lot of charges/prosecutions pending against the tribals under the Forest Conservation Act, 1980 and the Indian Forest Act, 1927 with retrospective effect.

There is no provision in the Act of 2006 that cases under the Forest Conservation Act, 1980 against the forest dwelling Scheduled Tribes for accessing minor forest produce would be dropped or closed. There are thousands of such cases pending and hundreds of plough and cattle remain impounded by the forest department officials. These cases are to be dropped or withdrawn by the government.

The same problems were projected on 25th June 2008 in a seminar convened by the Ekta Parishad attended *inter alia* by Chief Minister Shivraj Singh Chauhan, Principal Secretary, Scheduled Tribes Welfare Department, Principal Secretary, Forest Department and other service officers. It was alleged that "the forest officials were not accepting the applications for recording their names because the tribals have been encroaching upon the forest land for a long time."[2] Thus, the Act has yet to be popularized through wide publicity and training so that even the lowest level functionaries recognize the legal position. Some of the negative officials require punishment for their attitude.

There were large scale transfers of tribal land to the non-tribals. Even forest department got transferred about 1 lakh acres of tribal land through tribal agriculture societies. In districts of Gwalior and Morena, lot of Bhoodan Lands have been transferred.

Status of Alienation and Restoration of Tribal Land

As per Government of India's Department of Land Resources, Ministry of Rural Development Report, the position in September 2008 was as below including Chhattisgarh.[3]

- **Number of cases filed in Courts—53,806**
  Area 1,58,398 acres
- **Cases disposed of by the Courts—29,596**
  Area 97,123 acres
- **Cases decided in favour of tribals—21,834**
  Area 67,862 acres
- **Cases in which land was restored to tribals—21,834**
  Area 67,862 acres
- **Cases pending in Courts—24,210**
  Area 61,275 acres

The cases pending are huge involving 61,275 acres. These are either in revenue courts or with officers under the Tribal Department. A special drive and fixing up of responsibility for non-disposal or delay in disposal can ease out the situation. Cases rejected against the tribals should be re-examined by superior officer or group of superior officers. Responsibility should be fixed for rejection or disposal of cases against the poor tribals. Appeals or review in suitable cases should be filed. The revenue courts should follow the dictum of the latest amendment in the Code of Civil Procedure (Order XVII Rule-I), wherein not more than three adjournments should be granted to a party in a case. Rules should be framed by the Government of Madhya Pradesh so as not to allow more than three adjournments in a case of restoration of land to the tribal. More officers should be deputed for this purpose exclusively. The courts should also ensure that the tribals are given possession of the land simultaneously and the other person is paid due compensation on behalf of the government.

As regards Bhoodan Land, 31,000 acres of land is still to be distributed in addition to 92,000 acres available land ceiling surplus land which is of good quality cultivable agriculture land.[4]

Suggestions

Madhya Pradesh Government has hardly done anything on the distribution front of government waste-land and is one of the lowest in the country though the State has the largest geographical area in the country. Only 1,34,178 acres of land has been distributed by September 2006.[5] The Government of Madhya Pradesh should awake and do the needful *inter alia* to distribute government waste-land among the landless persons giving priority to the tribals and should take following steps:

1. The provision of conversion or diversion of agricultural land for non-agricultural purposes must be done strictly before the transfer or land acquisition so that tribals get partial advantage of enhancement of rate of compensation on this basis.
2. The land records should be updated in tribal pockets on priority basis and Gram Panchayats may be authorized to appear on behalf of the tribals to certify occupation if the tribal raiyat or landholder doesn't appear during Khanapuri-Bujharat operation or later on during hearing before the survey and settlement authorities.
3. The Bhoodan Land, government waste-land, Gaon Sabha land/Poramboke land have been encroached by the powerful landowners. They should be evicted and such land should be distributed to the tribals and other weaker sections of the society.

4. The non-irrigated or otherwise Banjar land distributed to the tribal beneficiaries should be provided with irrigational facilities or the land should be reclaimed or developed under various schemes of the Rural Development Ministry, Government of India like 100/150 days labour employment scheme known as MNREGA or various schemes under Integrated Tribal Development Programme (ITDP) where lot of surplus funds go back to the Government of India as unutilized. The popularly known 100 days or 150 days employment scheme has the biggest contribution to increase the daily wages in tribal areas. Thus, government schemes have salutary contribution which should be exploited and these schemes should be properly and honestly implemented.
5. The Gram Sabha is vague. It should be Gram Panchayat of the Gram Sabha. Secondly, effective functional committee is at the Panchayat Samiti level sub-committee which is missed in the Act. This gap should be filled in.
6. The ownership of minor forest produce has been unequivocally provided in PESA in 1996 and also in STORFA. This proposition has been pursued variously in different States ever since the consensus reached in State Ministers Conference in 1976 as a part of tribal sub-plan strategy.

Conclusion

It is hoped that Naxalism will be fully brought under control if foregoing suggestions regarding tribal land are taken into consideration and adequate measures are taken to plug loopholes in land laws specially relating to tribals.

REFERENCES

1. Saxena, NC: "Forests and the People Policy Issues in Madhya Pradesh" in *Land Reforms in India*, PK Jha (ed), Sage Publications, New Delhi, 1993, p 337.
2. *Dainik Jagran:* Hindi daily newspaper published from Bhopal, 26th June 2008.
3. Annual Report (2006-07): Government of India, Ministry of Rural Development, p 260.
4. Ibid, p 256.
5. Ibid, p 255.

7

Tackling Naxalism in Bud in Karnataka

The Naxal movement in Western Ghats (Karnataka) surfaced for the first time in 2003 when there was exchange of fire between Naxals and police near Kudremukh. Later on in Udupi district, Left Wing activist Parvathi and Hajime were killed by police in an encounter. As a revenge, Naxals burnt Forest Department's Traveller's Bungalow in Nemmaru Shringeri taluka. In 2004, the Head Constable Muddappa was kidnapped by Naxals. In 2005, Naxal leader Saket Rajan alias 'Prem' was killed in an encounter. In contrast, Naxal supporters increased their violence and killed 7 policemen in Tumkur district by hundreds of Naxals. In 2005, there were eight Naxal incidents causing 6 deaths.[1] In 2007, Congress leader Venkatesh was killed by Naxals. In November 2008, 3 Naxals were killed in Chikmagalur district and Constable Guruprashad also died in an encounter. In December 2013 Union Home Ministry sent an advisory to the Karnataka Government that CPI(Maoist) were trying to open a new theatre in South India. Thus, the Naxalite movement is grouping and re-grouping in Karnataka and sporadic violence by Naxals surface here and there. It has affected districts of Mysore, Kodagu, Udupi, Chikmagalur and Shimoga. It is high time that Karnataka Government gears up to face the challenges posed by the Naxal movement. Some non-government organizations (NGOs) functioning in Naxal-affected areas say that the question of livelihood is one of reasons behind youths in the tribal areas embracing Naxalism. The tribals are being prevented from collecting minor forest waste (MFW) and some farmers are also being evicted from their small agricultural or horticultural land in the Kudremukh National Park (KNP) area in violation of STORF Act, 2006 promulgated by the Central Government. Implementation of land reforms is one surest way to tackle Naxalism permanently.

Flawed Land Distribution

The eligibility for the grant of land for agricultural purpose is:

(a) The person must have attained the age of 18.

(b) His/her gross annual income should not exceed ₹4,800 as per Amendment Act, 2003.

(c) He/she should either be a *bona fide* agriculturist cultivating land personally or have a *bona fide* intention of utilizing land for personal cultivation; and however, in case of the ex-servicemen and soldier, land may be granted if the gross annual income of the applicant does not exceed ₹12,000. The extent of land granted to any person should not exceed the prescribed limit, including land already held by him.

However, following reservation of land for distribution leaves no discretion with the local authority or Panchayat body to deviate in deserving cases:

(a)	Ex-servicemen and soldiers	10 per cent
(b)	Person belonging to the SCs and STs	50 per cent
(c)	Backward tribes	5 per cent
(d)	Political sufferers	10 per cent
(e)	Others	25 per cent

The salutary principle in land distribution is that the land should be given to the one who cultivates the land personally so that production increases. Land is not donation or gift. It is for landless people who are capable enough physically to cultivate land and have been habitually, traditionally or practically doing the job of cultivation. Allotment of land to ex-servicemen and political sufferers is now out of context. The priority list for distribution of land should be ideally laid down as follows like in West Bengal:

(i)	First priority	Landless Scheduled Tribe
(ii)	Second priority	Landless Scheduled Caste
(iii)	Third priority	Landless cultivator

(iv) The ceiling for allotment of land should be one acre. Persons who already hold less than one acre of land may, however, be given land to an extent which is equal to the difference between one acre and the land already held by them.

(v) In case of a sharecropper or tenant, half of the land cultivated by him as a sharecropper is taken into account in computing his total land up to one acre.

(vi) The Sthayee Samiti or sub-committee on land of the Panchayat Samiti at the block or taluka level may advise local revenue official in the matter of allotment.

(vii) No settlement of land is to be made with a person who is employed in a business, trade, undertaking government service or industrial occupation etc.

Thus, general cultivators will come under consideration after BPL category. STs and SCs are considered first for allotment of land. These BPL category list of persons is ready-made available at each Panchayat level and can be used to draw up priority list for allotment. First preference is to be given to the person in possession of land but only up to one acre of land. In that case, he will get priority even over and above Scheduled Tribe and Scheduled Caste cultivators or agricultural labourers or the landless persons as because disturbance in possession may lead to a war between the two poor persons which is not the aim of the land reform measures.

As the allotment of land and delivery of possession delink the allottee from the landowner who is also his moneylender, the financial institution like banks, cooperative societies or service-cooperatives should immediately step in otherwise he will again mortgage the land to the erstwhile landowner.

A survey by IAS probationers of the Lal Bahadur Shastri National Academy of Administration brings out the following fallacies in land distribution in Karnataka:

(a) The norms of allotment in about half of the quantum of land allotted have been violated.

(b) The package of economic assistance along with land allotment was lacking.

(c) The encroachment of land mainly in Bangalore district has been done by the powerful and ineligible persons.[2]

It is high time that injustice done to the underprivileged persons should be undone by giving them government surplus land. They should, in a big way, be assisted for crop finance loan on concessional rate of interest and government subsidy or schemes to reclaim and develop their barren or waste-land through various water harvesting schemes including under MNREGA.

It is surprising to note that as of December 2007, about 1,15,765 acres of land was not distributed out of a total area of 2,41,710 acres of land which is the poorest performance among all States (as per GoI report).[3] Even before taking over possession, lot of land got involved in litigation. This shows utter callousness. The vesting of land and taking over possession are simultaneous processes. At least paper possession is taken by the government which is also provided generally in most of the land reform legislations. One fails to understand what State Government of Karnataka has been doing with 45,343 acres of land pending in 1,505 cases at the High Court of Karnataka which is the highest in the country. Even in revenue courts 15,682 acres of land is locked. Karnataka is the first State to set-up the Land Tribunal which should be an alternative to the High Court but cases were not transferred to the Karnataka Land Tribunal. At present, unfortunately, Land Tribunals are scrapped. It is not understood why 38,008 acres of land is not being distributed which is held up for miscellaneous reasons. Failure of the State Government in this most important field of land reform gives ample reason why the Naxalism is raising its head in otherwise peace-loving, pro-administration, prosperous and IT leader State of Karnataka.

Government Schemes

Karnataka has done well in promoting distribution of homestead plots as per study conducted by the Rural Development Institute, New York, USA now known as LANDESHA. These homestead plots up to 15/16 decimal have been successfully used for vegetable and fruit cultivation and partly evergreen cultivation. These plots at least save the beneficiaries from starvation and put stability in their minds. This scheme is known as Ashraya and even Panchayats are purchasing land from free markets and are distributing among the landless persons from minimum 2,178 sq ft to 6,544 sq ft. This scheme deserves serious consideration and should be dovetailed with the Indira Awaas Yojana of the Ministry of Rural Development, Government of India.

Karnataka has also done well by distributing 13.72 lakh acres[4] of government waste-land which requires to be developed further through various government schemes like MNREGA or liberal financial grants or loans.

Tenancy Reforms

Karnataka is in line with at least seven other States in India which have banned land tenancy. After conferment of ownership on about 6 lakh tenants,[5] the State is resting on its laurels that it has done whatever was required for the tenant or the sharecroppers. But, in fact, informal tenancy exists all over the State. The tenancy that persists in the field is concealed/ oral and the names of tenants are not entered in the revenue records. In 1981-82, 6.04 per cent of the operated area was leased-in in the State despite legal abolition of tenancy. The average area leased-in by the tenant was 4.76 acre.

The study by IAS probationers[6] shows that of all tenants, 62.5 per cent have leased-in on sharecropping terms, 22.9 per cent on fixed cash rent terms, and 14.6 per cent on fixed rent terms in kind. Similarly, of the total area leased-in 59.6 per cent is under sharecropping, 21.6 per cent under fixed rent terms in kind, and 18.8 per cent under fixed cash rent terms.

In a survey of agriculturists in Karnataka in 2000, the Rural Development Institute, Bangalore[7] found:

1. 45 per cent of the respondents answering definitively state that tenancy prohibitions should be lifted.
2. 94 per cent of respondents answering definitively state that existing tenancy restrictions harm the landless.
3. 38 per cent respondents answering definitively report that at least one farmer in their village keep land fallow rather than renting it out because renting may lead to the loss of such land.

Benefits of Relaxation

There is a need for changing the existing tenancy prohibition policy in Karnataka into one regulating it instead of banning it. Such regulating law will have, as revealed in other States, more beneficial effects, the significant ones being:

1. removal of tenancy ban makes land available for the landless poor to cultivate, at least as tenants;
2. relaxation of prohibition allows lease of land for more productive use, diversification of agriculture and contract farming;
3. tenancy regulation provides tenure security to cultivators and regulates rentals and brings in transparency;

4. tenure security enables tenants to borrow credit, obtain input subsidies and other extension services easily;
5. tenancy relaxation eliminates fear of losing land left fallow.
6. Having achieved removal of exploitative intermediaries—Zamindars, Jagirdars and Inamdars—tenancy prohibition is no longer necessary. On the other hand, there is need to regulate commercial type of leases by companies to prevent 'new Jagirdars' converting farmers into 'new serfs'.

The informal tenants or sharecroppers on the pattern of 'Operation Barga' of West Bengal can be recorded.

Contract Farming

In Karnataka, the contract farming has given some good dividends specially in the field of exports of coffee, spices, fresh fruits, flower, cashew, vegetables, gherkins and raisins.

Some of the even marginalized farmers have made lot of money by adopting above types of crops and selling them through the corporate or agri-export zones. Gherkins alone has got ₹140-150 crore export markets every year. Rose and onion were exported from the State during 2005-06 for ₹50 crore.[8] The total area covered and the farmers involved in contract farming in Karnataka is still less then one per cent. In the meantime, the corporates have started seeking farmers to lease out their land which should not be permitted creating new brand of Zamindars and landlords. The experiment is to be kept under watch for some more years. If the benefits reach directly to the farmers in a substantial quantum, then the contract farming can be further promoted by relaxation of ceiling laws and tenancy laws on those farmers. It is still demanded from the corporate lobby that they may involve farmers whose land they have acquired not as daily labourers but as shareholders or individual owners in the form of cooperative farming or the registered society etc. If Naxalism spreads due to contract farming, then the contract farming will have to be discontinued.

Updation of Land Records

Karnataka is the leader in this field and has been awarded by Government of India in this regard. Karnataka has good revenue set-up and the machinery is quite motivated. It is estimated that all records-of-right along with maps of plots of individual raiyats or owners have been computerized in Karnataka and people can have most updated records-of-right. Thus, it is clear that Karnataka can venture successfully to bring about all types of land reforms to tackle the problem of Naxalism in the State.

Conclusion

1. The balance ceiling surplus and government waste-land should be distributed without further delay giving top priority to the Scheduled Tribes specially in the Naxalite affected areas/talukas of the State.
2. The priority list for the land reform beneficiaries needs suitable amendment. Land is for those who cultivate land personally.
3. The existing tenancy prohibition policy should be changed into agency regulation policy.

4. Informal tenants or sharecroppers should be recorded in Karnataka on the pattern of 'Operation Barga' in West Bengal and Land Tribunal should be again made the final appellate tribunal.
5. The scheme for distribution of homestead-cum-kitchen garden plots requires further encouragement and patronage by government and Panchayats.
6. Extensive schemes should be implemented for reclaiming and developing waste-land, government land also by dovetailing various rural development schemes.
7. Efforts have been made to link up transfer of land through registration with updation of land records through normal processes of mutation and conversion. Karnataka should attempt to give maps of plots along with the records-of-right or copy of Khatian with respect to village boundary and adjoining plot configuration as is being experimented in West Bengal. This will combine best points of both raiyatwari system in South and permanent settlement system in rest of the country.

It is hoped that the good network of revenue and settlement administration will soon tide over temporary show of discontent in the form of Naxalism. The resurgent revenue administration led by requisite 'political will' will be able to contain Naxalism in the State.

REFERENCES

1. Government of India, Ministry of Home Affairs: Annual Report, 2007-08, Annexure V, p 143.

2. Lal Bahadur Shastri National Academy of Administration, Mussoorie, *Land Reforms in India, An Empirical Study*, 1989-90, Vol I, pp 75-76, 113-117.
3. Government of India, Ministry of Rural Development, Annual Report 2006-07, Annexure XLVIII, p 257.
4. Government of India, Department of Land Resources, Quarterly Progress Report for Quarter ending December 2007.
5. Ibid, Annexure XLIX.
6. Ibid 2, Table S T-1, p 7.
7. Jaamadar, SM: "Contract Farming in Karnataka: Its Implications for Policy" in *Contract Farming and Tenancy Reforms*, RS Deshpande (ed), Concept Publishing Co, New Delhi, p 152.
8. Ibid, p 144.

8

Tackle Naxalism in Uttar Pradesh in Advance through Implementation of Land Reforms

Naxalism is raising its head in some parts of the eastern Uttar Pradesh. Some of the modules of Naxalites have already been demolished by police. But the Naxalites are grouping and re-grouping in districts of Chandauli, Sonbhadra and Mirzapur.

One of the reasons of abject land discrimination in eastern Uttar Pradesh is that areas covered by Benaras State and Mirzapur South District were excepted from the ambit of Uttar Pradesh Zamindari Abolition and Land Reforms Act, 1950. Though these areas were later on included but the injustice to tribals already done could not be undone even today. In Banwasi Seva Ashram case in 1988, this point was raised before the Supreme Court but the problem is still not solved. NTPC unit in Mirzapur district is still holding lakhs of acres of land in excess of its requirement by misusing the Land

Acquisition Act which is also causing law and order problem in the area as land grabbers and mafia have become active in the area. Naxalites are showing it as justification for their movement in the area.

Uttar Pradesh is the most populous State in the country. As one of the pioneer States in the field of land reforms, the Government of Uttar Pradesh enacted the Uttar Pradesh Zamindari Abolition Act, 1950 which prohibited leasing of land except in special circumstances like the disabled persons, defence service personnel, widows and minors. As a result, the tenancy nearly came to an end. Sharecropping of course, exists in all States of India. West Bengal recognizes it in all its aspects and about 15 lakh sharecroppers have been recorded in West Bengal. Even in Bangladesh and America, sharecropping is recognized. If self-cropping is agreed to be the best alternative, let us accept that in most situations, sharecropping is the second best alternative.

With the changing times, Uttar Pradesh revenue administration had to realize the need for change of their approach towards tenancy. In fact, in Uttar Pradesh, the hidden sharecropping is rampant. The person who cultivates the land of another person on Adhia, Batia or Bhag is called sharecropper. In Uttar Pradesh, there are millions of instances where people are leasing out their land for cultivation. The transactions are like ordinary business transactions for a season, for a year or more. Seeing these types of cultivation in Uttar Pradesh, one tends to support contract farming though contract farming is anti-farmer and it has to be adopted only in a limited way in a well-defined conditional environment.

As per field survey done by me during 1990-92 and recorded in the book *Land Reforms in India:*

> "There are approximately 16 per cent sharecroppers in Uttar Pradesh. Thus, there will be about 30.37 lakh unrecorded tenants in Uttar Pradesh on total 87.85 lakh holdings (1991)."[1]

However, from 1981 to 1991, there was an increase of agricultural labourers to the tune of 25 lakh. This is very serious. The reason partly is that the unrecorded sharecroppers are driven out of their fields and they then have no other alternative except to resort to daily labour. The average acre leased in by pure tenant is 0.61 ha.

Recording of Sharecroppers in Uttar Pradesh

Within the framework of existing laws, the sharecroppers can be recorded in Uttar Pradesh in the following procedure:

> Under Section 33-A(2) of the Uttar Pradesh Land Revenue Act No 8 of 1977, the provision has been substituted as under:
>
> > "The provisions of Sub-Section [1] shall *mutatis mutandis* apply to a person who has been admitted as a Sirdar of any land U/S 195 of the Uttar Pradesh Zamindari Abolition and Land Reforms Act, 1950, before the commencement of the Uttar Pradesh Land Laws [Amendment] Act, 1977 or as a Bhumidhar with non-transferrable rights under said section after such commencement, or as an Asami of any land U/S 97 of the first mentioned Act."

The State should arrange for recording of Asami on a large scale as a policy as Kanungo and other lower officers will not be able to face the powerful lobby of landholders in villages. This can be achieved on the same pattern as 'Operation Barga' in West Bengal.

Distribution of Government Surplus Land

Uttar Pradesh lags behind in distribution of land. Though, it is one of the largest States in the country, only 2,63,225 acres of agricultural land could be distributed out of 3,39,385 acres of land available for distribution. Total number of beneficiaries are 3,03,867, whereas in West Bengal total number of beneficiaries are 28.5 lakh.

Land under litigation is about 50,000 acres. And waste-land distributed is 24.89 lakh acres as per 2006-07 report published by the Ministry of Rural Development, Government of India in April 2007.

There is lot of hunger for land in Uttar Pradesh and number of agriculture labourers is gradually increasing.

Many of the assignees of government-vested land ie Pattadars have not yet got actual possession of their land and erstwhile powerful landowners continue to get that land cultivated by their musclemen. Encroachments should be immediately removed from their land held by Pattadars by the respective District Magistrate. Some of the Pattadars or AVLs have not cultivated their land because institutional finance is not available to them. As a result, they have leased out their small parcels of land to other farmers having means and resources for cultivation.

This doesn't mean that the State should encourage leasing out by these poor men. On the other hand, State should arrange crop financing to them at a concessional rate of interest (4 per cent or less) so that they can cultivate their land by their own labour which is the greatest satisfaction for a villager. Contract farming can never be another alternative for these poor farmers. It will mean that the State wants to increase the number of landless persons and agricultural labourers.

According to a Chinese proverb, the number of times a farmer puts his foot on his land, production will increase Naturally, a farmer will visit his own field. One cannot go and trespass land belonging to another person. Owning land gives so much satisfaction and security to the poor person that he puts best of his labour and attention to the land. Labour constitutes 30-40 per cent as input in agriculture. As a result, the production increases automatically. Secondly, there is no other alternative employment available to this army of unemployed persons in rural areas. Even today there are about 27 per cent persons below poverty line (BPL). They require land to take benefit under some scheme or the other of the government. Banks will not allow any credit to the persons below poverty line (BPL) unless they have land which is an identity for a villager. Simultaneously, developmental schemes like MNREGA, ITDP should be used to develop land.

Out of 96.36 per cent persons found in possession of land, only 66.59 per cent were recorded in revenue records as per survey in 1992. This gap needs to be filled-up immediately. The ceiling limit for irrigated land with two crops is 7.30 ha, for one crop 10.95 ha and for dry land it is 18.25 ha. This should be reduced to 5 ha, 7.5 ha and 12 ha respectively and process of vesting should go on. Exemptions of religious and charitable trust from imposition of ceiling, exemptions of groves and Abadi, Benami transactions, transfers by the adverse possessions, arithmetical mistake, incorrect compilation of 61-B (total landholding of a person in Uttar Pradesh), Hibba name by Muslims and problems in the definition of family, were some of the reasons behind failure of land ceiling. Complications in deciding ceiling limits for various qualities of land and defining family, lead to prolonged trail of cases, leading to higher possibility of mischief. Many people were shown 'dead' before 1973 on the basis of certificates given by Gram Pradhans. Many divorces were obtained on paper, many children were adopted and many other children were shown to be adults on the basis of 'Farzi Parivar' register. Performance of Uttar Pradesh regarding the imposition of ceiling on landholdings has not been very satisfactory. The 1960 Act could not cut much ice. So it was drastically modified in 1973. But by the time of the coming of 1972 Act, only 2.87 lakh acres out of the estimated 7.50 lakh acres have been declared surplus.

Due to delay in allotment, allottees are unable to take effective possession of the allotted land. Land Army should be constituted to take over possession of Patta land by Pattadars like in the previous regime of Mulayam Singh government. Land is sometimes not allotted to deserving persons. In courts, State is represented by Naib Tehsildars, who very often are not aware of the up to date position of laws and rules and also are no match to the lawyers engaged by parties in marshalling laws and evidence. Minor officials are at the mercy of influential large landowners. Land allotted is more often Usar and Banjar.

Weaker sections are not organized and are not vocal. Supervision of senior officials is slack. Loopholes in ceiling laws are also required to be plugged. There should be no relaxation of ceiling limit for religious or charitable trust or Wakf, endowment or institution.

Conclusion

State of Uttar Pradesh is at a critical juncture. The poor people have asserted and the new government has been installed. State of Uttar Pradesh had to do away with Uttarakhand because the ZA and LR Act 1950 was not applied there.

Similarly, some exemptions were made in Mirzapur South District and Benaras State. Now, Naxalite agitation is raising up its head there. State owned Nazul Land is also excepted. And it is a bone of contention and source of corruption. Land reform is the best solution to the problem of Naxalism which is rising in Uttar Pradesh.

It is, therefore, suggested that serious attention should be given to implement the twin measures of land reforms ie recording of sharecroppers and distribution of government surplus land. Political will as well as administrative will are required to take Uttar Pradesh into new era of agricultural production and egalitarian society by implementing land reform measures.

REFERENCE

1. Agrawal, Dr PK: *Land Reforms in Uttar Pradesh*, MD Publications Pvt Ltd, New Delhi, 1993, p 170.

9

How Naxalism was Tackled in Andhra Pradesh?

Andhra Pradesh has since been divided into two States namely Telangana and Seemandhra in 2014. All the nine districts of Telangana are affected by the Naxal violence whereas four districts are in Seemandhra i e Srikakulam, Vijayawada, East and West Godavari, and Visakhapatnam districts. In Telangana, five districts are very badly affected i e Khammam, Karimnagar, Warangal, Adilabad and Nalgonda. However, the basic problem as regards Naxalism and land laws continue to be the same.

Erstwhile unified State of Andhra Pradesh topped the list of Naxal violence in the country.

During 2006-07 only, new States of Chhattisgarh and Jharkhand have overtaken Andhra Pradesh.

What Went Wrong

Andhra Pradesh used to be one of the better organized States from land reforms point of view after independence. There is a good political party organization as well as a good revenue set-up. Therefore, we shall examine in details as to what has gone wrong on the basis of figures below:[1]

	2003		2004	
	Incidents	Deaths	Incidents	Deaths
(1)	(2)	(3)	(4)	(5)
Andhra Pradesh	577	140	310	74
India	1,597	515	1,533	566

	2005		2006	
	Incidents	Deaths	Incidents	Deaths
(1)	(6)	(7)	(8)	(9)
Andhra Pradesh	535	208	163	43
India	1,608	677	1,272	610

Most tenancies in Andhra area are based on oral contracts. Barring a few cases, the land records are scarcely a guiding factor in determining as to who the tenant is.

> "A comprehensive law on the ceiling on agriculture land holdings was enacted and brought into force in Andhra Pradesh in 1975. At that time, it was, estimated that over one million acres of distributable surplus land would be available. But the State Government could take over only 0.54 million acres. What more significant was that 0.258 million acres got caught in litigation at different stages. Every declarant, who could afford it, moved the court. Often enough title verdicts favoured them. In the course of these ponderous litigations, several appeals which the government decided to file could not be filed and where

> matters were carried to the Supreme Court, they found themselves in a queue of appeals and revisions which would take years to resolve."[2]

In Andhra Pradesh 'standard holding' range is from acres 10 to 27 wet and 35 to 54 dry. No scientific study has gone into the determination of a 'standard holding'. The State has enough problems to contend with in regard to agriculture land ceiling schemes. If the State Government manages to bring to some conclusion the litigation pending in courts, substantial area will be available for distribution.

Concealment of Surplus Land

Another bane of the land reforms legislation has been the concealment of surplus land by the declarants. Unfortunately the Act does not provide for a 'review' of the closed cases when any concealment is detected. Attempt has been made to correct this infirmity through legislative action. It is also proposed to provide for voluntary declaration by landowners if they had concealed any surplus land. Such declaration would save them from the punitive actions provided in the Act.

Most tenancies in Andhra Pradesh area are based on oral contracts. Barring a few minority of cases, the land records are scarcely a guiding factor in determining as to who the tenant is. The Protected Tenancy Act was introduced in Telangana area in 1950. But 6 years previous to it, government ensured that the occupation of the land by the tenant was properly recorded in the land records which eventually became the basis on which the tenants were properly recorded in the land records and his legitimacy was established. For historical reasons, it was not so in Andhra Pradesh area. However, now a consolidated Andhra Pradesh Land Licensed Cultivators Act, 2011 has been enforced which allows all the tenants who are not registered to take advantage of crop loan and for that purpose they can be temporarily recorded and certificates can be issued to them by the revenue authorities. This is quite a pragmatic approach to the problem.

The State Government having been fully conscious of the strong emotional attachment of the tribals to the landed properties, have accorded utmost importance to the problems of alienation of tribal land in the Scheduled Areas. Special Regulations were made in exercise of the special legislative powers conferred under Fifth Schedule to the Constitution of India. The Regulations provide for the prevention of alienation of tribals land, and for restoration of the illegally alienated land.

The Regulations prohibit several forms of transfer of land such as sale, lease, gift, mortgage, exchange etc in favour of non-tribals. Whenever a transfer of land is made in the scheduled areas, it should be only in favour of a tribal or registered cooperative society consisting of only tribals. To support this measure, the Regulations also prohibit registration of transfer deeds unless the transfer is in favour of only a tribal or an exclusive tribal society.

Non-Tribal Issues

A special machinery has been created to implement the regulation effectively and to evict the non-tribals in illegal occupation of tribal land and also to restore such land to tribals. The regulations also seek to pursue such non-tribals who acquire land in contravention of the regulations or who continue to remain in occupation of the land even after they are evicted by the authorities with rigorous imprisonment for a period, are unique in the country in as much as they prohibit transfer of not only tribals or their exclusive cooperative societies. This measure ensures prevention of the alienation of land which the non-tribals illegally acquired from tribals in violation of the legal provisions. The regulations do not affect the legitimate family partitions. Similarly, inheritance by succession is also not affected on account of the regulations.

Recognising the position that the indebtedness of tribals, the government has brought about debt relief regulation and moneylending regulations for redeeming the tribals from being in debts, and to control and regulate private moneylending.

Besides, the State Government has also recognized the need for the survey and updating of land records in the scheduled areas effectively combating the problem of tribal land alienation. Three special survey divisions with full complement of staff have been established for undertaking this task in parts of the scheduled areas where the problem is more acute.

In Andhra Pradesh, different provisions of land reforms are applicable to different regions. In Andhra areas, the old Act of 1950 was repealed and a new Act—Andhra Pradesh (Andhra Area) Tenancy Act, 1956 was enacted. Similarly, tenancy reform in Telangana is guided by the Tenancy and Agricultural Land (Validation) Act, 1961. The Telangana Act recognizes temporary, leasing for six years which can be again renewed for the same period. A family holding in Telangana area varies between 4 to 60 acres.

Ceiling Limits

The Andhra Pradesh Land Reforms Ceiling on Agriculture Holdings Act, 1973 prescribes ceiling limit. The ceiling area of the family unit was fixed as equivalent to one standard holding with a maximum of 2 standard holdings for a family unit in excess of 5. In 1977, the Act was amended which allowed one additional standard holding for each major son. Nearly 4.45 lakh declarations were filed in the State but only 13.53 per cent declarations were decided as surplus and remaining 86.4 per cent were decided as non-surplus. It is learnt that the State is trying to have a re-look to rejuvenate land reforms set-up. At least, pending cases could be decided and possession to assignees of vested land would be given and updated land records will be handed over to each person. For that purpose, the government has already passed the Andhra Pradesh Rights in Land and Pattadar Pass Books Act, 1971. Until the 1966-67 rising in Srikakulam in Andhra Pradesh, the general belief was that rural India has always been a mass of sleeping villagers acquiescing in every form of injustice. The Telangana Movement was aimed at restructuring agrarian social relations through direct action against the government. The government was thus, obliged to embark upon a radical land reform policy to wean the peasants away from militancy. The Telangana region has a high proportion of tenancy due to the prevalence of pervasive absentee landlordism.

The first round of land ceiling in Andhra Pradesh in 1961 was an abysmal failure. Only about 7,400 acres of land became available and very little land could actually be distributed to the poor against the estimated target of 30 lakh acres of land.

The Predicaments

In Andhra Pradesh, the informal tenancy persists even in Telangana area where leasing is not permitted. The landless tenants are in a bad shape. The land taken on lease by them keeps them at below subsistence level. The landowners frequently change their plots. They are mostly sharecroppers. They meet the entire cost of cultivation and receive less than 50 per cent share of produce.

Several anomalies still persist. To identify and detect informal tenancy by the administrative machinery hardly exists. The provision of conferring the status of occupancy tenants to sharecropper/tenants-at-will is under neglect. The right of continuous resumption without any time limit, provision of surrender, and loose definition of 'personal cultivation' continue to be the loopholes in the tenancy provision of the State. There is domination of big farmers like politicians and merchants. Exemption of cash plantation from ceiling laws requires discontinuation. At least, it is hoped that the aforementioned problems be sorted out to some extent by the Act of 2011 after its due implementation.

The Way Out

The ceiling laws are very generous and they should be brought at par with other States as per the guidelines laid down by the Government of India. Restriction of right of transfer of land in Telangana by the tenants for institutional credit is depriving the cultivators of land. There should be training of revenue officers. There should be formation of new land tribunals.

Functioning of taluka level review committee relating to land reforms should be geared up. Updation of land records in the State is much required. The definition of 'Personal Cultivation' is vague. The Tenancy Act should recognize oral agreements. The Tenancy Act should recognize oral agreements, the burden of proof should rest on the landowner not only in the context of fixation of Fair Rent but also in respect of all other matters like 'Personal Cultivation'. Tenancy reforms can be implemented only through Revenue Department and all disputes relating to such matters should be adjudicated by competent revenue official. The jurisdiction of the judicial officers should be restricted. The right of resumption seriously affects security of tenure. It should be abolished.

The rent is still on the high side. It should be fixed at 1/5 of gross produce. Encroachments on government land should be removed and surplus land should be distributed among the landless or poor cultivators. Priority should be given in distribution of government-vested land to those eligible persons who are already in possession of land and are cultivating the same. The tribal land illegally transferred should be restored to the tribals. Informal sharecropping or tenancy should be recorded only up to the life time of the sharecropper unlike in West Bengal, which is heritable. Thus 15-30 per cent of total owned land can be recorded under tenancy without any ownership right only for right of cultivation by the tenant. The Andhra Pradesh Government has constituted a special task force to tackle Naxalites' menace called Greyhounds. Apart from one or two setbacks, the Special Task Force has performed well. The permanent solution lies in implementing land reforms with due sincerity and political will. If some of these suggestions are implemented in true spirit in a time-bound fashion, Andhra Pradesh and Telangana will come out of morass of Naxalism soon.

REFERENCES

1. Government of India, Department of Land Reforms: Quarterly Progress (Cumulative) for the quarter ending December 2007).
2. Agrawal, Dr PK: *Land Reforms in States and Union Territories in India*, Concept Publishing Company Pvt Ltd, New Delhi, 2010, p 104.

10

Bihar: Lack of Willingness

Bihar is the biggest State affected with Naxalism. It is competing with Uttar Pradesh in lawlessness. Various governments have come and gone but problem of Naxalism exists in Bihar. While one travels through Bihar, one doesn't know when his train will be derailed by the Naxalites, killing or injuring him. Such a situation cannot be allowed to exist for long.

When one talks to a police officer in Bihar, he says that the defective land records generate armed struggles. The politicians feel that historical abject poverty is the cause of Naxalite violence. The administrators attribute interference by the politicians in law and order machinery. The social activists assign lack of involvement of people like that of Panchayat etc or NGOs in Bihar. Outsiders feel that irresponsible politicians have caused such state of affairs in Bihar.

There is no denial that first term of Nitish Kumar government from 2005-2010 was a great hope for people. But that government also didn't touch the long-term solution of land reform in Bihar in spite of having a solid mandate from the people. D Bandyopadhyay Commission was set-up for the purpose but most of the recommendations of the Commission to implement land reform have not been implemented till date. The political executives feel that land reform is a Pandora's box. If they open, they will not be able to handle it. But that is the only solution. Government has to take a risk to tackle this all pervading problem to achieve a long-term solution of complex problems of Bihar which will also pave way for placing development on fast track.

There is plenty of scope to improve things in the area of land reforms in the State. If the records-of-right are updated in Bihar and are published, many of the genuine grounds of Naxalism in Bihar can be obliterated. The status of main component of land reforms in Bihar including Jharkhand ie vesting of ceiling surplus land and its distribution among the beneficiaries is as follows as on 30th September 2006 (in acres)[1]:

Area declared surplus	*Area taken possession*	*Area distributed to individual beneficiaries*	*Total number of beneficiaries*
4,15,447	3,90,752	3,06,964	3,79,528

There is hardly any improvement afterwards.

No Records

The problems were many. The information about the total land information about the total land including those in Benami names with the ex-Zamindars is not statistically available. Besides Zamindars succeeded in keeping 14 per cent to their estate in the form of Khas possession which nobody could touch. As per estimates of the Revenue Department of the

State, the total land in Khas possession of the ex-Zamindars would be to the tune of 15 lakh acres.

In addition using unscrupulous methods, such as Benamadari, collusion with revenue officials and politicians, coupled with their social status and power, the ex-Zamindars of Bihar succeeded, by and large, in protecting their class interests. The examples are there for everybody to see. The ex-Zamindards of Darbhanga, Hathwa, Dumraon and Ramgarh still own large tracts of land. Even tenure holders under them, like Raghubans Narain Singh of Kursela, happens to be a big land-owner. Maul Babu who once prided himself on being a modest raiyat of Raj Darbhanga, now possesses around 18,000 acres of land and an air strip!

It is clear that Bihar is lagging much behind in vesting of surplus land. In West Bengal 5,36,912 tribals got land as Pattadar whereas in Bihar only 43,050 tribals got government land. This is the quantum of problems in Bihar and Jharkhand which are witnessing large scale extremists' activities. On the other hand, out of 86,291 cases filed for restoration of alienated land of tribals, only about 50 per cent cases ie 44,634 have gone in favour of the tribals.

However, there is still lot of scope to distribute the remaining government land and 1.56 lakh acres of Bhoodan Land among the tribals on priority apart from lot of government waste-land which is yet to be distributed. Even consolidation of land holdings of 96.05 lakh acres of land was tilted in favour of landowners. Therefore, it was stopped from 1992. It is not understandable why the consolidation operation has started once again in Bihar wef 15-3-2004 without streamlining revenue administration.

The second biggest bottleneck in land reforms measure is non-recognition of sharecroppers in Bihar. As per report of Government of India, in September 2006 total number of tenants conferred ownership rights were not reported. West Bengal achieved magical feat by recording 15 lakh Bargadars or sharecroppers without conferring ownership right on them. They only share 50 per cent share of produce if the owner gives plough, cattle seeds, manures, fertilizers and other inputs. If the sharecropper provides all inputs for cultivation he would get 75 per cent share of produce. The latter is only on paper but the right is there. If West Bengal can do it, why the adjoining State of Bihar cannot do it having the same system of land records and system of permanent settlement. Only little more initiative and political will are required for this purpose.

Denying Rights

The landowners are tactfully utilizing judicial proceeding to deny rights to the poor cultivators and are taking undue advantage of the corrupt and demoralized revenue machinery. They even go to West Bengal and take some order of stay or injunction on the pretext of title suit and prolong suits for years. As a results, the poor cultivators lay down their arms and morale and leave everything on destiny. For past few years, they have now started taking recourse to Naxalite elements who protect them from undue exploitation and injustice and take revenge on the Zamindars by way of armed attacks for their annihilation. The landowners have also organized themselves. Therefore, it is no longer one way running over the others. It is only violence which comes on surface in which police and administration are dragged as law and order maintenance agency. Then, the movement of Left

Wing Extremists (LWE) get diverted towards the police force and their main focus is lost. It is violence, murder and forceful occupation of land all-round and no permanent solutions come forth. The land which was once forcibly taken in possession by the LWE, is recaptured by the landowner with the help of police force as the law of land is in their favour. Thus, correction and updation of land records become very crucial in Bihar for launching land reform measures. Let us examine how best the old and outdated records-of-right in Bihar can be updated.

Hoghwash

Khanapuri (filling up the records) is the most critical stage in the survey operations. The rest of the stages involve database created. The matter of creating record should not be left to the Amins. From the initial stage, the revenue officers or Naib Tehsildar can be associated with this work so that at later stages of attestation and objections, there may not be many objections. At local stage, there should be transparency. Even the representatives of Panchayats should be given notice to be present. The objection should be decided at the Khanapuri Attestation stage and only objections after final publication should be invited. Three stages objections thus should be reduced to two only or even one. It is learnt that the survey and updation of land record work in twenty districts is underway in Bihar. This should be completed at the earliest in all districts.

Inadequate Staff Strength

The survey and settlement wing is inadequately staffed. In West Bengal, there are about 30,000 employees and officers whereas in Bihar, there are not more than 10,000 staff and officers. Government of Bihar has to carry on the burden with its own resources to increase staff. But this is worth. This is the basic responsibility of the State Government which they should discharge if they have to stay in seat of power otherwise disgruntled public led by the extremists will run over their ivory towers.

Ideal Records as Reality

Andhra Pradesh has shown that the registration wing of government can be linked with the revenue or land reform wing. No registration should be done unless the records are seen as correct on computer. After registration, the records can be simultaneously corrected. Thus, there will be automatic system of updation of records-of-right. The fees for mutation and conversion can be duly charged at the common service centre as done in Madhya Pradesh, Andhra Pradesh and Karnataka.

Once the maps are digitized, the raiyat can be given his records-of-right along with map of plot boundaries with respect to the village. This will be the best and the final records-of-right which will have no lacuna or gap. This records-of-right will have all god qualities of ryotwari settlement in south India. The 'recording of rights' operation should be conducted in the mission approach on the pattern of 'Operation Barga' in West Bengal.

Legal Measures

Under Section 44 of the present Bihar Land Ceiling Act, it should be obligatory for the State Government to prepare and publish revised records-of-right. Therefore, instead of the word 'may', the word 'shall' should be substituted in that section. This will provide a legal basis for annual updating of records which should be done on regular basis.

The provision of consultation with landlord for subletting the land should be done away with because it practically amounts to giving the landlord the right to change his tenants. The implementation of the maintenance of Land Records Act, 1973 should be taken up in the right earnest in blocks affected by Naxal agitation. The laws relating to land reforms should be codified in one single statute. The names of encroachers should not be recorded.

Administrative Measures

A separate machinery for implementing land reforms should be set-up and selected officers may be put on the job. There should be regular training of officers in order to equip them with the requisite knowledge of the laws, rules, regulations and various instructions issued by the government from time to time. Executives instructions should be reiterated so that the police officers should be bound to follow the orders of the revenue authorities in these matters and assert their authority in the interest of the allottees of the surplus land and Bataidars or sharecroppers.

Construction of the office-cum-residences for lower revenue functionaries in the Tolas of the weaker sections of society will instil greater confidence and bring justice to their doorstep.

The provision of Section 71(a) of the Chhotanagpur Tenancy Act (CNT Act) should be enforced strictly so that land belonging to the members of the tribal community may be restored to them. The number of appeals and revisions should be restricted to just one in order to avoid vexatious litigation.

Field visit by the original court should be made a mandatory provision in all restoration cases. Restoration register along with supporting records should be maintained at Halka/Anchal/sub-divisional level.

A time limit should be prescribed for all recording operations, say one year. A 'Rakma-Milan' with the previous survey should be rigidly adhered to so that the alienation of tribal land is not regularized. The recording officer should not be allowed to open Khatas in respect of such land in the name of non-tribal which have been recorded in the name of tribal in the previous survey. Annual computation sheets (rent-rolls) should be regularly prepared and updated.

Officers who have already done their district tenure, should be posted as settlement officers in those areas.

There should be special squad at the disposal of the Deputy Commissioner/District Magistrate for giving possession of land to the tribal and the landless.

Bandyopadhyay Commission[2]

Government of Bihar had set-up a three-man commission chaired by D Bandyopadhyay who had spearheaded Barga recording operation in West Bengal. It is learnt that the Commission has given its report which *inter alia* contains recommendations on strengthening administration of land revenue set-up, upgradation and computerization of land records and recording of informal tenants or sharecroppers.

The government is still examining the report after many years.

I met the then powerful Chief Minister Lalu Prasad Yadav twice and requested him to implement land reforms in Bihar as he had people's mandate. He referred me to his close associate Prem Chandra Gupta who didn't understand land reforms. Then, I met the Principal Secretary of the Government of Bihar on the issue. According to him, due to internal dissension, government in Bihar will not be able to take up implementation of land reforms. I hope that Government of Bihar overpowers the land lobby in Bihar to usher Bihar in a new era of progress and prosperity and save the State from disaster.

REFERENCES

1. Annual Report 2006-07, Government of India, Ministry of Rural Development, pp 255, 256 and 257.
2. Internet.

11

Naxalism and West Bengal

It has been proved beyond doubt that one of the repercussions of non-implementation of land reforms was the growth of 'Naxalite' movement. The surfacing of the Naxalite movement in 1967 in West Bengal and its positive ending by the Left Front government in West Bengal by implementing land reform measures has proved this case in point very clearly. It again reappeared in West Bengal in 1971 and was tackled in 5 years. It again reappeared in the year 2009 and disappeared in 2012 after the death of Naxal leader Rao in police encounter.

The Naxalites or the CPI(ML) introduced a distinct style of peasant warfare, with its distinct ideology and strategy. This movement more than any other created panic in public because of lot of violence and bloodshed.

> "The basic thrust of the movement is to focus attention on the grievances of the people, inequities suffered by large segments of the population, release of victims of exploitation from the tentacles of the landlords, etc and to inculcate 'class' responsibilities among the economically and socially deprived

> sections. In pursuance of these objectives, the groups have not only mobilized the people but have also ensured that distributive justice is available in a rough and ready manner. The peoples' courts organized by these groups expropriate surplus land from the landlords to be distributed to the landless, dispense criminal justice, settle disputes and punish offenders. Thus, 'Jan Adalats' constitute a cornerstone of their efforts to win over the masses, particularly in the rural areas. Besides, they indulge in extortion from businessmen, contractors, traders, government officers, etc and resort to murders and kidnappings to eliminate interference by agents of the established administration and defiant class enemies."[1]

In the last movement, the Naxalites concentrated more on corrupt Panchayat leaders of the ruling CPI(M) and murdered an ex-district head of Panchayat in Purulia district and a Gram Panchayat Pradhan in East Midnapur district because they were coming in their way to spread their influence in villages. Many of these murders where initially appreciated by public because the Panchayat office bearers had made lot of fortunes and erected multi-storey buildings which were eye-opener to the villagers and they supported the Naxal cause.

The movement did not bring any immediate results in West Bengal and was short-lived but had far-reaching implications and became a force behind numerous peasant struggles in different areas of West Bengal, Bihar, Jharkhand (by tribals), Chhattisgarh (by tribals), Andhra Pradesh and Punjab. However, the Left Front government led by CPI(M) in its three successive terms, starting from 1977, salvaged the situation by recording about 15 lakh sharecroppers known as Bargadar under 'Operation Barga' programme. This was consolidated by proper distribution of surplus land to the landless and by providing bank credits. For example, up to 1978, in six years total 74,000 people got crop finance whereas in the year 1979 alone 59,000 got crop finance. Thus, the Communist government in West Bengal had consolidated its position, which was envied by even Central Government and other State Governments.

Measures Taken

In West Bengal, the implementation of land reform under the Left Rule from 1977 has stabilized the rural society eg the average size of land holding was 0.99 ha in 1976-77, which has come down to 0.82 ha in 2000-01. The land held by marginal farmers has increased. In 1976-77, the land held by marginal farmers was 14.18 lakh ha whereas in 2000-01 it had grown up to 27.59 lakh ha. Similarly the land held by small farmers has also grown up from 14.9 lakh ha to 16.07 lakh ha, whereas the land held by the semi-medium and medium farmers has been reduced to less than 50 per cent, whereas in case of large farmers, the total available land is negligible ie 2.19 lakh ha. Similarly there is an increase in cultivated land by SC and ST marginal farmers. The total land operated by SC marginal farmers in 1995-96 was 5.33 lakh ha whereas in 2000-01 it became 6.5 lakh ha. It was 1.85 lakh ha for ST marginal farmers in 1995-96 whereas it increased to 2.07 lakh ha in 2000-01 whereas in case of large ST farmers, it has become 0 from 530 ha in 1995-96. Similarly, considerable reduction in area cultivated by semi-medium and medium farmers belonging to SC and ST farmers is observed. Cases of SC and

ST show that the land reform measures have really benefited the lowest strata of the society socially and economically. Even the ownership of land in case of SC and ST marginal farmers has increased. In 1995-96, 81 per cent SCs were holding land whereas in 2000-01, 85.4 per cent SC marginal farmers were landowners. In case of ST, 77.17 per cent marginal farmers were there, whereas in 2000-01, 80.42 per cent marginal ST were the land holders. The number of large holdings from category of semi-medium and medium consequently have been considerably reduced. In fact the ST large farmers have become nil. It shows that there is a peaceful revolution. This has also been reflected in increase of area cultivated by SCs and STs. In 1995-96, 48.67 per cent area was cultivated by the SCs whereas in 2000-01 the area cultivated was 60.11 per cent of arable land. So also in 1995-96, 47.4 per cent ST population of marginal farmers cultivated land whereas in 2000-01, 52.33 per cent of ST marginal farmers cultivated the land.[2] Thus, land reform measures have created the basic stability in the rural society of West Bengal. As a result, the Naxalite movement can't have its permanent setting in West Bengal. However, there are stray movements in the State by extremists for the following factors:

- Discrimination by the Panchayat bodies in distribution of fruits of rural development schemes.
- Neglect of the area being far-flung from the main stream of development.
- Increase of awareness of rights among the neglected rural population specially STs.
- Lack of education and lack of health facilities in these areas as compared to other areas.

- Non-effective participation by the ST representatives because of their simplicity in the functioning in grass root level decision-making bodies regarding rural development schemes specially Panchayats.

Tenancy Recorded

West Bengal is the only State in the country, which has recorded about 15 lakh Bargadar on about 11.1 lakh acres of land. There is hardly any recording of sharecroppers in other States. They just want to overlook the issue showing that there are actually no sharecroppers, which is not a fact on the ground. Haryana had 18.22 per cent land under tenancy in 1981-82 whereas West Bengal had only 12.34 per cent land under tenancy and Haryana has not recorded any sharecropper. Similarly, total land in Uttar Pradesh was 10.24 per cent under tenancy as per NSS 1981-82 figures whereas the recording of sharecroppers is negligible. There is no problem if there is no tenancy like in Gujarat (1.9 per cent) and Kerala (2.05 per cent). Average number of tenant in a village in West Bengal is 50, whereas in Uttar Pradesh it is 14 and in Tamil Nadu it is 20. Frequency of change of plots is almost negligible. In West Bengal 97.09 per cent tenants do not change plots whereas in Uttar Pradesh 47 per cent tenants do not change plots. Tamil Nadu is another State which shows 95.97 per cent stability of plots with tenancy whereas in West Bengal 20.3 per cent STs are tenants. It means from tenancy point of view also, there is stability in rural West Bengal. On the order hand, unrecorded tenants were noticed in the villages of Bihar as 95.36 per cent, Uttar Pradesh 87.29 per cent and Haryana 57.8 per cent.[3]

Distribution of Surplus Vested Land

West Bengal is the leader in the country in respect of distribution of vested land. The State has distribution of almost 22 per cent of the total surplus land distributed in the country to almost 53 per cent of the total beneficiaries i e Patta holders who are 29 lakh on an area of 10.23 lakh acres as per reports published by Government of India, Ministry of Rural Development. Similarly land has been distributed to about 3.16 lakh poor families for homestead purpose involving a quantum of 18,989 acres of land. Perusing above, we find that land reform provides basic stability in the State. The distribution of government surplus land slowed down after 2005 because the Left Front government had become complacent because of their long rule in the State from 1977 and the vested interest exercised their influence on government functioning. However, some committed officers at the helm of affairs like Land Reform Commissioner (LRC) continued to implement various components of land reforms including distribution of land in the worst Naxal-affected areas in spite of threat to him. Naxalites ganged up with the powerful opposition party in the State and provided their fire power to fight against long rule of the Left Front government which resulted into various inter-party fights. And the opposition party could fight back the powerful cadres of CPI(M) in 2006-07 culminating into Nandigram police firing in which 16 people died.

In the later phases of the land reform, the administrators continued allocating the vested land in smaller parcels. Given the fact that large numbers of landless are not owning even a very small parcel of land, this implementation of policy made good sense.

A Practical Case

During the high level meeting at the State level, the plan of action was drafted to distribute most of the remaining government-vested land to the really deserving landless beneficiaries irrespective of party colour or affiliation. It was pointed out that the joint field verification of land along with the Panchayat functionaries takes time. To tackle this problem, instructions were given to do field verification by government machinery only with district administration i e revenue inspector at the Gram Panchayat level. The list of proposed beneficiaries was also traditionally submitted by the Panchayat functionaries. It was changed as BPL (Below Poverty Line) lists were readily available at block and Gram Panchayat level. Out of those, landless persons were to be identified first. Priority was given to ST and SC landless BPL families or persons.

A time-bound programme was chalked out and Director of Land Records and Surveys was asked to monitor the progress of work. Officers from Directorate of Land Records and Surveys were also deputed in three affected district of West Medinipur, Bankura and Purulia. They were asked to visit those three districts and affected blocks and guide the field functionaries to expedite preparation of case records for final decision by the Land Sub-Committee (Ban-O-Bhumi Sanskar Sthayee Samiti) of the Panchayat Samiti. Final gearing up was done by fixing the Patta distribution camps at selected places where dignitaries or VIPs would attend the programme of distribution of land. The first such camp in the worst affected block was attended by LRC himself. This energized local level machinery. This also expedited the decision-making by Panchayat bodies and sub-divisional officers who had not been attaching so much importance to the job.

One Patta distribution camp was even attended by the Chief Minister himself. Other ministers including Minister of Land and Land Reforms of the Government of West Bengal attended Patta distribution programme. Senior officers attended the programme where Ministers were not available. This has generated confidence among tribals and others who were feeling neglected due to apathy of their Panchayat representatives who were again very simple people. They could not overcome obstacles created by the middle class bureaucracy armed with feudal rules and regulations in the rural development works. It was ensured that the deserving persons get Pattas. This generated confidence and support in the masses residing in far-flung areas of the State who have become supporters of Naxalism. They came in great numbers in these camps. Wherever land was not available, government implemented another land distribution scheme by purchasing land from the open market with State Government funds. Rest of the things were done by departmental funds of Public Works Department and 12th Finance Commission to construct roads in these inaccessible areas.

The correct message has also reached the local rural development administration including Panchayats that they have to function without fear and favour. The political will also was clearly demonstrated by the top government functionaries and ministers attending to the land reform programmes.

REFERENCES

1. Agrawal, Dr PK: *Issues in Land Reforms*, Rajiv Gandhi Foundation, New Delhi, 2000, p 12.

2. Agricultural Census Report 2000-2001 for State of West Bengal (Summary), Land and Land Reforms Department and Directorate of Agriculture, Government of West Bengal, December 2005, p 28.
3. Iyer, Prof K Gopal: *Land Reforms in India*, Vol I, published by Lal Bahadur Shastri National Academy of Administration, Mussoorie, 1989-90, p 157.

12

Exposition for Naxalism in Maharashtra

In Maharashtra, district Gadchiroli adjoining Naxal-affected State of Chhattisgarh is always in news, regarding Naxalite violence. As per recent records available, 400 persons have been killed in three decades. Few of the recent records are as follows:

February 2014	:	7 Naxals killed in police encounter.
May 2014	:	12 policemen killed in mine blast.
September 2014	:	4 policemen injured.

It is very surprising and shameful how such a slaughter of human beings is being carried out in such an advanced State of Maharashtra. The Government of Maharashtra is unable to solve the problem of Naxal violence in one district for the last 30 years. It means that the solution of Naxal violence is somewhere else i e in implementation of land reforms.

Blockages

The implementation of land reforms in Maharashtra is beset by bottlenecks. The execution of agrarian reform laws was periodically reviewed by the State Government and the first such comprehensive review was undertaken as far back as in 1972. The only intermediary tenures that are being continued today are the Devasthan and Wakf Inam grants.

Abolition of intermediaries resulted in the conferment of occupancy rights on a very large body of under-right holders and some tenants in all parts of the State. This could indeed be said to be the first major step towards the transition of a feudal order to democratic social order.

The Maharashtra Agricultural Lands (Ceiling on Holdings) Act 1961, came into force on 26th January 1962. An area measuring 1,24,493 ha, was declared surplus under the provisions of the said Act.

> "The ceiling was lowered in 1975, as a consequence of which an area of 1,60,962 ha was declared as surplus. Out of the total area of 2,85,455 ha, 2,51,522 ha has already been distributed."

Land measuring 18,422 ha had to be excluded from distribution because this was either uncultivable or needed for public purposes or was involved in exemption claims. An area of 6,204 ha is involved in litigation.

Allocation

The proportion of Scheduled Castes and Scheduled Tribes land allottees in Maharashtra has been as high as 53 per cent. The ceiling which was initially imposed on agricultural holdings in 1962, was substantially lowered within a short span of just about 13 years.

The very fact that the land declared surplus under the Amended Act of 1975 were considerably more than what had been acquired under the Principal Act, is proof enough of the fact that the Act was implemented quite successfully in Maharashtra. Maharashtra's performance as far as the implementation of the Ceiling Act is concerned, therefore, speaks for itself. These ceilings will be further lowered with the passage of time by the operation of the laws of succession.

> "Maharashtra has distributed about 10.22 lakh acres of government waste-land but 77,000 acre of Bhoodan Land is still to be distributed."[2]

Tribal Land Alienation

The law relating to the prevention of alienation of tribal holdings in favour of non-tribals is sufficiently stringent in Maharashtra. Government has also taken steps to ensure restoration of land which had been transferred by the tribals in favour of non-tribals under due process of law to the tribals. Land measuring 43,351 ha (1 ha = 2.471 acres = 10,000 sq metres) have been restored to the tribals under these measures. Immediate concern is to augment the compensation admissible to the non-tribals.

Though, redistribution of the ceiling surplus land has gone a long way in the expansion of the owner cultivation by a 'politically costless' means unavailable to other crowded States like Kerala and West Bengal. This was the distribution of just over a million acres of cultivable waste-land.

However, it will be wrong to presume that the political leaders in Maharashtra had any intention or the political will to implement the land reform legislation seriously and honestly.

It is a well-known fact that in Maharashtra the dominant political class comes from the rich peasantry. The rich sugar barons control the political leadership of the State. Even the then Chief Minister known for his concern for land reforms, had spoken publicly for the economic, political and the administrative arguments for retaining the old ceiling limits in 1971. At the time, even the lower rank of hegemonic Congress Party in Maharashtra came in open revolt against the new ceiling law, to be promulgated and implemented. As a result, the Ceiling Act of 1975 (implemented in 1978) did not change the ceiling limit at 18 acres for the most valuable land (irrigated land). As the revenue department has become a general administration department, it has utterly neglected its original revenue work. The records were not updated. In backward and hilly districts, where Naxalites are active, neither the landowners nor revenue officers cared to record the changes in revenue records. As a result, the landlords as well as small and marginal farmers were harassed by the Talathis who are custodian of records-of-right.

If records-of-right are not up-to date, further land cannot be vested to the State nor Benami land can be unearthed. The poor people who were given Patta of government land were not recorded in revenue records. Thus, they were at the mercy of revenue officials (talathis) or the erstwhile landlords who continued to occupy their entire land though it got vested to State by law.

Tenancy Reforms

The tenancy legislations are different for the three regions of Maharashtra. The Mumbai Region is covered by the Bombay

Tenancy and Agriculture Land Act, 1948 and (Amendment Act, 1955); the Marathwada region is guided by the Hyderabad Tenancy and Agriculture Land Act, 1950, the Bombay Tenancy and Agricultural Act, 1958 (Vidarbha region and Kutch area) applies to the rest. The provisions of each are similar. They provide for fixity of rent, security of tenure and compulsory transfer of land to the tenants which are non-resumable by landlords.

State of Maharashtra gives two extreme situations. In Vidarbha region sharecropper or the landless person feel deprived of their rights whereas tenant in Pune, Kolhapur belt is sometimes richer than the landowner himself. Most of them have been working with their landowner for more than 10 years. The tenants after the 'Tillers Day' were entitled to purchase the tenancy within one year. The government run co-operative farm under Maharashtra State Farming Development Corporation in Pune demonstrates an ideal system where the individual partner can retain the ownership and can cultivate collectively. The cause of disparities in various regions in Maharashtra requires a close look. The experiment has been done in Maharashtra itself. The problem is to undertake the implementation of this successful experiment to all parts of State without caring for political backlash. Then, only the extremist movement which is raising head here and there can be tackled effectively and its further spread can be checked engulfing other regions of Maharashtra which happen to be one of the richest and most forward-looking States in India.

> "As in September 2006, 14.92 lakh tenants, have been conferred ownership rights on 42.90 lakhs acres of land which is better figure than West Bengal."[2]

Following weaknesses or bottlenecks were further noticed in implementation of land reforms measures:

1. Absence of correct and updated records and lack of knowledge on the part of sharecroppers to know the details of land, they cultivate.
2. Lack of financial support for land reform beneficiaries. As a result, they take refuge of the local moneylenders who exploit them fully. And the moneylenders are not being punished under the Moneylender Act.
3. Weakness and irregularity of the reporting system and of evaluation.
4. Delay in disposal of cases by revenue courts as well as civil courts and the High Court.

Suggestions

1. After the 'Tillers Day', no attempt has been made so far to enrol the new informal tenants. A special drive should be undertaken to identify informal tenants and confer ownership rights on them.
2. The definition of 'tenancy' should be broadened so as to include cash rent/kind rent and crop shares.
3. No surrender of tenancy should be permitted as these surrenders generally are forged or are managed in an emergency situation of a tenant or a sharecropper.
4. In Vidarbha region, the resumption of land by the landowners for personal cultivation up to three family holdings (ie from 21 to 120 acres) should be reduced. The definition of 'Personal Cultivation' should not

include cultivation by hired labour under the personal supervision.

5. Tenants conferred with ownership rights have to be directly integrated with the anti-poverty programmes.

Acquisition and Displacement

In Maharashtra, the tribals are 9.27 per cent of the total population. But among those displaced people, the tribals were about 27 per cent. In 1979, Maharashtra had the largest number of large dams in the country i e 631 dams which were either completed or are in the process of being completed. This caused movement against dispossession of the land by the local tribal people. These tribals finding no satisfactory rehabilitation package took recourse to the Naxalism. Five rehabilitation schemes are there on papers but these are meant for the persons who can take advantage of the schemes. Illiterate and simple tribals cannot perhaps, take proper advantage of these schemes. As a result, they are denied their rights. After being lost their agricultural land and home, they have nowhere to go except to join Naxalite outfits. Thus, the resettlement and rehabilitation work under land acquisition schemes by the government should be given similar priority as land acquisition. Land should be handed over only after the resettlement issues are decided and finalized in the field and not only on the papers. This is a very strong dictum for the present day regulatory administration but the government has to choose whether they want to deliver fruits of development only to the few and leave the affected persons in lurch compelling them to join violent/armed outfits. On the other hand, the press, NGOs and armed groups are equally vocal and publicity-prone to ballooning these adverse effects of every development project. Thus, more caution and pro-active action is required on the part of the government as a whole. The Land Acquisition Act, 2013, if implemented in true spirit can solve the problem of resettlement and rehabilitation in future.

Co-operative Farming

There is a pro-active experiment going in Pune successfully for many years on the State farm under the Maharashtra State Farming Development Corporation.[4] The land is owned by the individual cultivators but arrangements are made for cultivation through modern implements and inputs collectively. The marketing is also done on co-operative basis. Thus, it is the ideal system of cooperative farming keeping individual ownership intact.

Conclusion

Though the incidents of Naxal violence are increasing in prosperous State of Maharashtra, yet everything is not lost. Maharashtra has lot of resources of fund and personnel. The political will and administrative will are required to be made operational. It seems that in its march towards industrialization, Maharashtra is forgetting its poor people who feed large cities and big towns. Time is ripe to take a re-look at the implementation of land reform measures along with making minor legislative amendments here and there. The revenue administration is to be given top priority, which was given during seventies. If the development schemes are not implemented or made operational, the land acquired should be returned to the tribals or at least unused or excess land should be returned to them. Panchayat bodies are to be geared up and they should be co-opted in the process of land distribution and even in recording of sharecroppers. The tribals and poor cultivators in Vidarbha and Marathwada regions should be given institutional finance i e bank loan for cultivation on concessional rates so that they do not have to commit suicide. Rate of suicides is the highest in Vidarbha, Maharashtra. Bank credit for crops, crop insurance and simultaneous punishment to moneylenders can extricate the situation to a large extent. Large number of suicides by farmers speak poorly of the performance of land reforms in the State. Let this blot be removed and Maharashtra should lead in the field of land reforms as in the past.

REFERENCES

1. Agrawal, Dr PK (2000): *Issues in Land Reforms*, Rajiv Gandhi Foundation, New Delhi, p 44.
2. Ibid, Annexure XLVII, pp 256 and 257.
3. Annual Report (2006-07): Government of India, Ministry of Rural Development, Annexure XLIX, p 258.
4. Agrawal, Dr PK (1993): *Land Reforms in India*, MD Publications, New Delhi, p 231.

13

Frequently Asked Questions: Decoding Naxalism

Q 1: What is Naxalism?

Ans: 'Naxalism' or 'Naxalite' words are derived from Naxalbari in district of Darjeeling in West Bengal where there was a struggle in 1967 against the government authorities with the avowed object of capturing power through violent revolution.

Naxalbari is 6 kms from Nepal, 22 kms from Bangladesh, 120 kms from Tibet and was surrounded by thick forests and tribal population of 1,26,000. The movement started with the seizure of land and murder of few landlords and class enemies, i e landlords, bureaucrats etc. The movement was led by late Charu Mazumdar, Secretary General of Communist Party of India (Marxist-Leninist).

Q 2: What is the basic thrust of the Naxalites?

Ans: The basic thrust of the different outfits of Naxalites is to focus attention on the grievances of the people, inequalities suffered by large segments of the population, focus on few poorest of the poor due to their exploitation by the rich persons, their success stories of release of victims of exploitation from the tentacles of landlords and inculcating 'class' responsibilities among the economically and socially deprived sections and punishment of class enemies like landlords, government officers, contractors, leaders of ruling party by way of direct action by them. They aim to establish a classless society based on egalitarians principles and revolutionary struggles. Resorting to violence remains the cornerstone of the major Left Wing Extremist (LWE) groups known as Naxalites in India with a lot of underground and over-ground cadres and supporters. The major Naxalite groups are People's War Group (53 per cent) and Maoist Communist Centre (MCC) (30 per cent) apart from other splinter groups. They believe that power emanates from the barrel of the gun. Unless the existing system is overthrown, no worthwhile results can be expected in favour of the deprived sections of the society.

Q 3: What are sources of fund of Naxalites?

Ans: The main sources of income of Naxalites are:

1. Ransom after kidnapping of government officials or local rich people.
2. Usurpation of land of rich landowners and allotment to their supporters and taking share in production.
3. Collecting subscription from the local people by bringing them to their fold.

4. Realizing the proceeds by giving forest or government land on lease.
5. Taking levy from rich persons and traders.
6. Selling forest or mineral produce lying in government stackyards.
7. Realizing levy from government officials and officers.
8. Forcefully imposing commissions from contractors of government works and Panchayat functionaries.
9. Outside help and assistance.
10. Realizing levy on raising local mineral resources by the industries or traders.

Q 4: What are the most affected areas of Naxal violence in India?

Ans: Naxal activity affects about 40 per cent of the country's landmass and about 35 per cent of the total population. The Naxalites are now well-entrenched in the States of Chhattisgarh, Jharkhand, Odisha, Andhra Pradesh, Telangana, Bihar, Madhya Pradesh, West Bengal, Maharashtra, Karnataka and a part of Uttar Pradesh. The Naxalism now has affected about 183 districts in 11 States. The number of districts affected by Naxalism is on the decline. In fact, fully Naxal-affected districts are 76 only.

As per figures published by the Ministry of Home Affairs, Government of India, from 2003 to 2008 (6 years) the incidents of Naxal violence were increasing involving more casualties as below:

	Total (6 years)	Average per year
Number of Incidents	9,403	1,567
Number of casualties in civilians	2,871	479
Number of casualties in Security forces	982	164
Number of Naxalites killed	892	149

Thus, a day doesn't pass when the Naxal violence doesn't take place. The extent of Naxal violence is more than the violence by the terrorists as Naxal violence is well-spread and is unpredictable.

The averages of incidents and deaths from year 2010 to the year 2014 are 1904 and 684 respectively showing that though the incidents are increasing yet due to better police action, number of deaths is on decline from 792.

Q 5: How do the Naxalites function?

Ans: The major organization People's War Group (PWG) has organizational set-up from Central Committee, Special Zonal Committee (at the State level), regional committee, divisional committee, area committee and down to the village committee. The next Maoist Communist Centre has three frontal organizations namely—(a) Party organization, (b) Force/army organization and (c) People's organization.

These organizations have various fronts of farmers, labourers, women, young persons, students and of intellectuals. There are two other well-known Naxalite organizations ie CPI(ML) (Vinod Mishra) and CPI(ML) Party Unity (PU). CPI(ML)(VM) is well-equipped with men and arms, yet it believes in taking part in election process. Sometimes, some splinter groups all of a sudden appear on scene causing a big incident of violence.

The Naxalite outfits believe in publishing their ideology so that people in large number may be associated with their organization. They usurp the movable and immovable properties of the capitalists. After taking possession of land of big landowners, they allow their members to cultivate that land under their direct patronage. They even realize levy from the landowners.

Once they take local public into confidence, they declare any area as guerrilla zone and administer that through their supporters by giving them armed protection. If the police force comes to intervene, they utilize land mines to cause large number of casualties to the security force and loot police arms and ammunition.

They occupy government vacant land, forest land and Benami land. They hold people's courts in villages and settle local disputes amicably or deliver forced justice on the spot. They enrol disgruntled unemployed youths by convincing them about failures of government. They also kidnap officers to pressurize local administration. They burn down roadways buses, railway stations, telephone centres and towers, Panchayat Bhavans, school buildings, rural roads, mining site, forest roads and culverts and even cause explosion on railway tracks. They sometimes attack police station and commit jailbreak. They call bundhs to show their strength. They extort money from the landowners, moneyed men and contractors.

They hire young villagers to come to their fold by offering them monthly remuneration or by giving them financial assistance apart from brainwashing them into their ideology.

They have their selected training centres in the dense forests. They publish magazines and literature regularly. They run their organizations efficiently and there is no dishonesty in running their organizations.

Q 6: What are the ways and means to defeat Naxalism?

Ans: The ways and means to tackle Naxalism are twofold:

(i) Police Solution

(ii) Development Solution

The law and order solution or fire fighting solution by security forces will include encounters, arrests and detention of Naxalites, interrogation of Naxalites, arrest and detention of associates, helper, collaborators, and financiers of Naxalites, intelligence collection and using modern sophisticated countering strategy. The non-police or development solution will *inter alia* include implementation of extensive land reforms viz distribution of land to the landless tribals in their villages or in their vicinity etc, development of roads and other rural development schemes like MNREGA, Indira Awaas Yojana, ITDP, implementation of the Scheduled Tribes and other Traditional Forest Dwellers (Recognition of Forest Rights) Act, 2006, winning of hearts and minds and brainwashing them, restoration of governance in Naxal dominated areas, rehabilitation of the surrendered Naxalites as per promise.

When both strategies will work in unison, the Naxal problem can be tackled.

Q 7: What is 'Operation Green Hunt'.

Ans: The term 'Operation Green Hunt' does not exist in any official record. This is the name given by the local Superintendent of Police, Chhattisgarh for local security force operation with an aim at busting Naxal dens in Bastar Forests existing in green camouflage. There is no speciality about this. Police generally gives a strategic name of any long-drawn police operations to streamline them.

Q 8: What is the government policy to combat Naxalism?

Ans: The Central Government has adopted an integrated four-point approach to address the Naxal problem in the areas of security, development measures, enforcing rights and entitlements of local communities, public perception management and good governance.

All stakeholders including the State Governments were consulted before finalizing the National Policy and Action Plan.

Q 9: Do the Naxalites have links with other terrorist organizations?

Ans: Some of the Naxalites arrested have accepted that they had close ties with many North-East insurgent groups, especially the RPF/PLA of Manipur. They have links with Nepalese Maoists. Most of these outfits have links with internal forces inimical to India. The Naxalites have also frequently expressed their solidarity with the J&K terrorist groups. Many a times, the supplies of arms from North-East insurgent groups have been intercepted by the security forces to the Naxal outfits in various States.

Q 10: What is the main problems in combating Naxalism by the government?

Ans: The Naxal violence has been viewed for a long time as a law and order problem only. Over the year, the Naxalites have increased their out-reach so as to threaten the internal security of the country. Therefore, it is an internal security problem being co-ordinated by the Central Government. Secondly it has been recently viewed as a developmental problem too. The governments have now initiated multi-pronged measures to address the deficit of development in the Naxal-affected areas. This has halted the expansion of Maoism in India. However, still the governments are not looking for its permanent solution which is rooted in implementation of land reforms which is a State subject.

It is hoped that the Central Government and the State Governments will reach to the root cause of the Naxal problem and will tackle the same earnestly.

Bibliography

Agrawal, Dr PK: *Issues in Land Reforms*, Rajiv Gandhi Foundation, New Delhi, 2000.

______: *Land Reforms in India*, MD Publications Pvt Ltd, New Delhi, 1993.

______: *Land Reforms in States and Union Territories in India*, Concept Publishing Company Pvt Ltd, New Delhi, 2010.

______: *Naxalism: Causes and Cure*, Manas Publications, New Delhi, 2010.

Gupta, Ranjit Kumar: *The Crimson Agenda: Maoist Protest and Terror*, Wordsmiths, Delhi, 2004.

Joshi, PC: *Naxalism: How to Cope With*, Kalpaz Publications, Delhi, 2014.

Kumar, Uday: *Defeating Naxalism: Ways and Means to Defeat Naxalism*, Lucky International, New Delhi, 2012.

Kumawat, ML and Dr Nazrul Islam: *Police and Naxalism: Strategies for Solutions*, Manas Publications, New Delhi, 2011.

Website: www.mha.nic.in as on 19th August 2015.

Index